GATEWAY
TO THE DAO-FIELD

GATEWAY
TO THE DAO-FIELD

Essays for the Awakening Educator

Avraham Cohen

CAMBRIA
PRESS

AMHERST, NEW YORK

Requests for permission should be directed to:
permissions@cambriapress.com, or mailed to:
Cambria Press
20 Northpointe Parkway, Suite 188
Amherst, NY 14228

Library of Congress Cataloging-in-Publication Data

Cohen, Avraham, 1942-
    Gateway to the Dao-field : essays for the awakening educator / Avraham
Cohen.
          p. cm.
    Includes bibliographical references and index.
    ISBN 978-1-60497-553-6 (alk. paper)
    1. Holistic education. 2. Education, Humanistic. 3. Reflective teaching.
I. Title.

    LC990.C64 2008
    370.11—dc22

2008031160

TABLE OF CONTENTS

LIST OF ILLUSTRATIONS

A FOREWORD WITH MORE THAN FOUR WORDS: NINE BRIEF RUMINATIONS AND ONE POEM

Carl Leggo

1

I am sitting in the palliative care unit of the Western Memorial Regional Hospital in Corner Brook, Newfoundland, Canada. My father is living and dying with a brain tumor that has stolen much of his speech and even more of his spirit. In this liminal space between living and dying, I am ruminating on memories, and experiences, and questions of love, relationship, ethics, and spirituality. And I am ruminating on the wisdom of Avraham Cohen's *Gateway to the Dao-Field: Essays for the Awakening Educator*.

2

My time with my father is drawing to a close, and my thoughts are focused almost entirely on living and dying, and the challenges that extend beyond a poet's imagination and resources. Reading Avraham's book, I am reminded that living is always a tangled story that often is, but never should be, taken for granted.

3

Avraham teaches me that the invitation we are offered with birth is the invitation to learn to live well, and to live well is to live with wisdom, and to live with wisdom is to live with a perpetual curiosity and courage and conviction. That is how Avraham lives.

4

Avraham holds fast to the conviction that our storied lives are never only unique and idiosyncratic accounts of individual and isolate experiences. Instead, our stories are always part of a network of communal and collaborative stories, a network that knows no beginning and no ending. As human beings, we are inextricably and integrally connected like fire and water and air and earth, sustained by an ecology of ancient elements.

5

Avraham's book is about living with wholeness and love in the world. This is Avraham's gift.

6

Avraham explores the places of dreams and visions, including the psyche, the inimitable imagination, and the ineffable heart. The inner life of the educator is a location that needs to be explored. Why are we reluctant to journey in the interior places—the less familiar places, the places for which we do not necessarily have well-prepared maps, the places where mystery reigns? We have so little experience with those places. Schools are not dedicated to exploring the inner lives of teachers or students. Avraham's book is; schools need Avraham's book.

7

Avraham's book is about healing, about the healing power of stories and sharing stories. Avraham understands "inner work for educators as a very important personal and spiritual process."

8

Perhaps lingering with the dying will help me learn living. We are all ill—living with death and dying. How then should we live? What does it mean to be human? Avraham understands "the importance of attending to the inner life of the educator in the service of living fully in-the-moment."

9

Avraham's book is a wise and poetic book—a book for savoring. This is a book about love. Avraham asks, "Is not true presence synonymous with love?" This is the fire in the heart of the book. This book can change your life. It is changing mine.

10

As a poet, I think every forward foreword should include a poem. So, I draw my ruminations to a temporary close with a poem about trout fishing with my father, not so long ago, now I know for the last time, a love poem about my love for my father and his love for my mother, all woven in a sturdy chorus of words that echo with Avraham's wisdom.

SKIPPER'S SECRET POND

trout are waiting, Skipper promised,
as we drove long around holes and twists
in the ancient logging road to his secret pond,
they're eager to meet us, Skipper assured me

even after seventy-six years he charged
like a rambunctious moose through
alders just a little less sharp than barbed wire
on a trail that didn't even exist except
perhaps in his inimitable imagination

I soon learned the secret of Skipper's pond
is there is no pond, more a marsh in a meadow,
a few scattered eddies like patches of skin
on a moulting caribou, and I told Skipper,
no wonder your pond is so secret

I caught a few trout, lost a lot more, my heart
is more in the romance of trout fishing than
playing Charon in the visceral liminal space
between squirming life and shriveled death

at days' end, with our quota of trout, most
caught by Skipper, we drove again the long
rugged logging road back to the highway

Skipper complained about hen-pecked husbands
who weren't allowed to go fishing because
they had to babysit or renovate or pick up
groceries, but he said about Carrie, Her and me,
we come and go, and every now and then, we
remember to thank the good Lord for one another

and I turned and saw a caribou chasing us
up Lady Slipper Road, gangly limbs blowing
in the July stillness like patio chimes,
and for a few minutes at least I knew
the secret of Skipper's Pond even if
I can't hold it fast, won't remember it long

Carl Leggo
Professor
Department of Language and Literacy Education
Faculty of Education
University of British Columbia
Vancouver, BC, Canada

FOREWORD:
EDUCATION AS AN
ENLIGHTENMENT PROJECT

Heesoon Bai

There sits Avraham, morning after morning, perhaps in the middle of
the night, too, in a light-drenched, large, windowed nook in the living
room of our small apartment, overlooking the busy city scene below and
the ocean and mountains in the distance. As a companion sitter, I hear
him sometimes intoning deep throaty sounds that resemble, to my ears,
Tibetan chants. This is a potent and unusual portrait of an educator:
someone who is greatly respected in his institution as a peerless teacher
of counseling graduate students. He is also a trusted and respected professional in the field of psychotherapy as a practitioner and scholar.
What does this sitter's—meditator's—portrait have to do with the field

of education? What does a person's contemplative practice have to do with teaching and educating?

Everything, if we consider educating as a process of helping individuals to become *fully* human, by which I mean 'enlightened' in the sense of Eastern enlightenment traditions. In *Education for Awakening*, Professor Yoshiharu Nakagawa (2000) speaks of Eastern philosophy having a "certain ontology that sees reality as a multidimensional, stratified structure and assumes the deepest dimension" (p. 18). Eastern enlightenment aims at waking us up into this multidimensional reality, which is the pathway to becoming more *fully human*. Sitting meditation, inner work, and other contemplative practices are the essential means that aid the awakening process.

Sleepwalking teachers cannot be models of awakening. If we want our students to be awakened to full reality and become more fully human, then it is essential that educators are engaged in the process of accessing this multidimensional reality. Now I better understand why Avraham insists on sitting every day on his meditation cushion, in front of the big windows, watching the crows and seagulls swoop by. To the extent he is awake, to that extent, he will be able to aid his students to become more fully awake. But what is this esoteric-sounding talk of awakening? Surely, I don't mean it literally. Or do I?

Avraham's book, whose manuscript I read many times over the past few years during its various stages and versions of preparation, addresses in detail (and in plainer language than I am couching here) what this awakening process is like, looked at from the humanistic educational perspective. Avraham came into the field of education through a circuitous path. He is an experienced psychotherapist and group facilitator, a potent educator of counseling students, and most centrally he is a facilitator of the process of awakening, which takes seeing psychologically how we became asleep in the first place. Being asleep means we are not in touch with reality as it is, and we may not even be aware that we are asleep. Psychologically speaking, we lose touch with reality when parts of us are denied, blunted, crushed, and shut down, hence we become *un*seeing, *un*sensing, and *un*aware.

In this book, Avraham with his acute psychological understanding documents how this process of shutting down and becoming numb typically happens. This process happens everywhere and anytime, from the earliest moment of our babyhood. When babies cry from distress, and parents do not attend to their needs because they are following family doctor's advice of scheduled feeding (thankfully, this is no longer the norm), or because the parents are too distressed themselves from overwork and a million other reasons, these babies begin to shut down in the face of what appears to them an indifferent or even hostile world. When well-meaning teachers continually demand—clamor for—students' attention in the name of instructing them, they are in effect impairing individual autonomy—the capacity to *be* oneself, to fully be *one with self.* Fullness of being does not flourish when attention is continually drawn away and drained out from self, as in conventional modes of schooling. Every time a person's sense of reality is invalidated or not recognized by another person, be it a parent or a teacher, parts of him or her shut down, even if only ever so slightly. Little by little, doors of perception close, and the person is incrementally and insidiously removed from reality.

For Avraham, education is an emancipatory project. Individuals learn to gradually throw wide-open shuttered windows and bolted doors that incarcerate their true nature. His philosophy and practice of education let in radiant warm light and vitalizing fresh air, and further the process of liberation for the authenticity of the individual and the classroom collective. It is the birthright of humanity to experience the full measure of radiance and bliss. So long, in the name of individual survival and social progress, much of both formal and informal education has functioned as an oppressor that, instead of liberating humans into more expansive and vital dimensions of Being, ends up creating one-dimensional devitalized beings whose hunger for fulfillment knows no bounds and no season, for we are starved of Beingness. We are the Hungry Ghosts in the Buddhist lore. Until we are awakened and opened, and can connect directly with the source of Being and Vitality, we are perpetually hungry and are driven to seek nourishment but in empty calories of success and entertainment. Can we radically reconceive education? In the pages of his book, education as enlightenment is what Avraham offers.

Avraham is inspired by the classical Eastern philosophies—notably, Daoism and Buddhism—and sees a great potential in them for turning education into an emancipatory project. However, here, we need to be careful to not confuse culture with philosophy. A philosophy loses its original soul and impetus when a culture seizes it and turns into an unconscious social force as dominant ideology, morality, and customs. Culture changes all the time, and soon the philosophy that once inspired the culture is forgotten or dismissed. Anyone who traveled to the Far East knows just how prevalent and vital Eastern philosophies are in these countries: not much. What Avraham is interested in is living philosophy. It is through pedagogical practice that centralizes the human dimension and its integration with curriculum that Avraham makes philosophy come alive, hence his daily sitting and engagement with other contemplative and inner work practices. These are my daily practices, too. As Avraham's partner in life and a fellow educator on the trackless path in the Dao-field, education as an enlightenment project is our mutual, cocreative work. We are together committing our lives to the project of elevating education to its proper stature and scope of enlightenment work. What this means is that he and I have to do our own enlightenment work—to become awake and aware. Indeed, we see our relationship as a crucible for our enlightenment work. This book that Avraham produced has been, through the transformative process in our relationship, crucible. Being intimately and integrally involved has been most exciting and personally gratifying.

In closing, I wish to draw the reader's attention to the significance of this work in the field of education. Today, education in the form of schooling, from kindergarten to university classes, is heavily focused on the transmission and transaction of content knowledge. There is nothing wrong with this focus, and it is a necessary focus. But what should be of concern to us is what is missing: primary focus on the quality of human beings. Avraham shows that education could and should play a major role in cultivating the fullest humanity.

In appreciation and hopefulness,

Heesoon Bai
Associate Professor
Philosophy of Education Faculty of Education
Director of Graduate Programs
Coordinator for Philosophy of Education PhD Program
Editor of *Paideusis: The Journal of the Canadian Philosophy of Education Society*
Simon Fraser University
Burnaby, BC, Canada

REFERENCE

Nakagawa, Y. (2000). *Education for awakening: An Eastern approach to holistic education*. Brampton, ON, Canada: Foundation for Educational Renewal.

ACKNOWLEDGMENTS

This book is based on my doctoral work in the Center for Cross-Faculty Inquiry in the Faculty of Education at the University of British Columbia. I am very grateful to those who helped shape that dissertation—in particular Dr. Carl Leggo, Dr. Tony Clarke, Dr. Karen Meyer, and Dr. Julie Diamond. I am also very thankful for the various grants, scholarships, and fellowships I received while working on this book, and I wish to thank the Social Sciences and Humanities Research Council of Canada, the University of British Columbia, and the Faculty of Education at the same university for their support. I am particularly pleased to have been awarded the Ted Aoki Prize for the outstanding dissertation in Curriculum Studies for 2006–2007 from which this book springs.

These acknowledgments would not be complete without mentioning my mother and father who gave me life and opportunity. In particular, I want to recognize my dad who told me, "The main thing that stops people is what they can think of. If you can think of it, you can do it." I have done my utmost to carry his message forward, and this book is a concerted effort in that direction. Acknowledgment of my grandparents, who voyaged across an ocean at the beginning of the last century, is central. Their pioneering spirit insinuated itself into me.

I also wish to recognize Dr. Peter Lavelle, my first mentor, who saw something in me at a time when no one else did and who had the courage to take a risk with me. I have attempted to return the favor whenever opportunity presented itself.

I want to thank my friends—Larry Green, Janos Mate, Hamid Moreau, Karen Fiorini, and my partner, Heesoon Bai—who provided Zen-like support to help me polish, ever-more finely, the final version of this book.

And, I want to acknowledge Auntie Evelyn for being who you are and whom you will meet more fully further along in the text.

Thanks to Gerda Wever of the Write Room and the Write Room Press in Burnaby, British Columbia, for her excellent advice and impeccable assistance.

Versions of some of the essays in this book have appeared and/or have been presented elsewhere. The essay titled *We Teach Who We Are and That Is the Problem* was presented at AERA 2005. My appreciation to the Canadian Journal of Counselling for permission to publish the essay titled *Classroom as Community: Deep Democracy Practice*, which was earlier published under the title *A Process-Oriented Approach to Learning Process-Oriented Counselling Skills in Groups*. The essay titled *Who's Different, Who's the Same* is reproduced with the generous permission of Springer Publishing Company (LLC, New York, NY 20035). It was originally published under the title *Dissociative Identity Disorder: Perspectives and Alternatives*. My appreciation to Constructivism in the Human Sciences for permission to reproduce the essay titled *Dreaming Life: Working With a Personal Dream—On My Own,* which was originally published in 2004 under the title *Working With a Personal Dream—On My Own.* Lastly, a version of the essay *The Inner Path and Outer Experience in Classrooms* was presented in 2006 under the title *The Secret Life of Educators and Students: What Actually Goes on in the Hearts and Minds of Classroom Participants, What It Means, and How to Work With It (and Not Against It)* at the

9th Annual Investigating our Practices 2006 Conference in Vancouver, British Columbia.

Thanks to Heesoon Bai for permission to use her photograph, *Traceless Blue*, on the cover of this book and to Lumina Romanycia for permission to use her photograph, *Friends*, at the conclusion of the book.

REFERENCES

Cohen, A. (2004, Fall/Winter). Dissociative identity disorder: Perspectives and alternatives. *Ethical Human Psychology and Psychiatry: An International Journal of Critical Inquiry, 6*(3), 217–230.

Cohen, A. (2004). A process-directed approach to learning process-directed counselling skills. *Canadian Journal of Counselling, 38*(3), 152–164.

Cohen, A. (2004). Working with a personal dream—On my own. *Constructivism in the Human Sciences, 9*(2), 49–58.

Cohen, A. (2005, April). *We teach who we are and that is the problem.* Paper presented at AERA 2005: Demography and Democracy in the Era of Accountability, Montreal, Quebec, Canada.

Cohen, A. (2006, May). *The secret life of educators and students: What actually goes on in the hearts and minds of classroom participants, what it means, and how to work with it (and not against it).* Paper presented at Investigating Our Practices 2006: 9th Annual Conference. University of British Columbia, Faculty of Education and British Columbia Teacher's Federation, Vancouver, BC, Canada.

INTRODUCTION

This book consists of scholarly essays that reflect upon human potential, particularly but not exclusively, within educational environments. The most important theme that runs through these essays is the need for an educational paradigm shift—away from centralizing curriculum and content and toward a focus on care and nurturance, as well as subjective and intersubjective understanding—a shift in which the educator is of central importance. This centrality means that educators must be supported, encouraged, and cared for in order to be best able to create conditions that will allow for the emergence of exceptional educational experiences for themselves and their students.

My approach to this paradigm shift is holistic, systemic, and based on the values of presence, care, and deep democracy. This approach prioritizes the person in educational environments. I have tried to show how personal experiences, including personal inner work, can and must be integrated with curriculum material. I have described inner work for educators as a very important personal and spiritual process and the integration of personal inner work, group leadership, and facilitation practice as central to extraordinary and profound educational experiences.

The ideas in this book are based on a variety of qualitative approaches, including living inquiry, autobiography and self-study, conceptual, narrative, poetic, auto-ethnographic, heuristic, and analytic methods. I have drawn upon philosophical and theoretical background from education, Eastern and Western philosophy, humanistic and transpersonal psychology, process-oriented methods, and counseling psychology. Yet most importantly, what is written here has come out of my experiences in the marketplace of my inner world, in the outer world, and in classrooms with students, where I investigated the material, personal, and ephemeral as integrated parts of the Dao-field of education and life.

GATEWAY
TO THE DAO-FIELD

Chapter 1

Path Lights

Opening
The Gateway opens
A subtle breeze comes through
The World changes,
Forever.
—Lao-Tzu's Mother[1]
—a. cohen

The Dao and Writer's States of Consciousness

I have been told at times by colleagues that they understand my writing because they know my work, but they are concerned that those not as familiar with me as a person and the way my mind works will not be able to comprehend what I am trying to convey. Perhaps this concern is valid—especially in the academic arena. Writing for me is not an engineering or architectural exercise. I am not trying to win an argument. Rather, I am trying to express what emerges, offer an opportunity, and share an alternative perspective. I am interested to reach toward the inner world of you, my readers. In the service of this undertaking, my intention is to write the way my consciousness actually flows, which just may be close to the flow (Csikszentmihalyi, 1997) that others are either in or looking for.

Daoist vocabulary offers another way to describe this state:

> *Dao* is an ontological notion: reality as a field of infinite possibilities of perception and action. In order to work in this field of possibilities, the human consciousness has to be receptive to the Dao, or, to be more accurate, it has to become part of the Dao. The mind has to become a microcosm of the *Dao-field*. (Cohen & Bai, 2007)

A Daoist way of being emerges over a lifetime of practice. Being in tune with the Dao in an educational environment means knowing in a substantial way what the context, content, and atmosphere of the environment are in the moment, each moment, with an awareness of what has been and what possibilities exist. The process is what is important, not in and of itself only but for the fullness of each step along the way and the learning that occurs through experiencing that process. From the Dao-field consciousness, ideas emerge that are felt as much as thought, imagined as much as described, and seen as much as dreamed. These ideas are like "impressions," different from abstract ideas that construct propositional statements. Impressions issue forth as if they are constructing themselves and have a life of their own. They seem to inscribe themselves into me. In fact, if this writing had emerged from everyday consciousness, characterized by calculations, lists, plans, anxieties in the moment and about the future, and daily events (not to disparage the important place that all these phenomena have in daily life), then it would fail to show and enact the significant coherence between form and content, medium and message. The words that you read are impressionistic inscriptions of my consciousness in the Dao-field.

My hope is that this book will encourage you to imaginatively try out ideas, and I hope that this will be an absorbing process for you. Optimal learning occurs when three major and integrated ingredients are present: It has personal meaning, it is experiential, and it has substantial content. My intent with this writing has been to engage these three dimensions throughout, and hopefully, I have succeeded with this undertaking.

HARD HEADS AND SOFT HEARTS: AN APPEAL TO THE READER

I recall years ago in a first-year English literature course learning that the idealists believed that separation of lovers was tragic while the romantics believed that, in these same circumstances, love was expanded. In education, educators continue to argue which of a variety of "realities" is better. I have witnessed "soft-hearted" pedagogues being torn to shreds by their apparently "hard-headed," critical colleagues. I have also seen the same soft-hearted pedagogues dismiss and ignore their hard-headed colleagues. What seems to be missing is acknowledgment that the skills and, often, the will to talk across this divide, or even to recognize that there is a divide, is lacking. In the end, the question as to which reality is true leads to division and alienation. Hard heads and soft hearts have something to offer, but the capacity to speak the language that crosses the divide seems to be missing. More importantly, the recognition and the connection between the human beings with these differing views are unacknowledged and lost, with resultant isolation, loneliness, and bitterness. Actually, the word *both* in reference to these views is far too narrow. Looking more deeply into what people are saying invariably brings out the otherness that exists even between those who apparently "speak" the same language. I use the word *language* here in the broadest possible sense. I am really talking about the capacity to appreciate difference not just in theory but in the crucible of dialogue. This can be very exciting, passionate, and difficult. Dialogue across the gap of otherness, diversity, and disagreement is an art that is nearly lost. Its recovery has great potential.

SIXTEEN THEMES AND IDEAS

The themes of authenticity, humane living, and ever-maturing creativity run throughout this book. Although my major focus is education,

I have included essays that are not directly about that subject, but which have a direct application to being human and the education of educators. These essays demonstrate the commonality of these threads in different contexts. These themes are important to how I live, teach, and practice psychotherapy. They describe the capacities that underlie whatever abilities I have to deal with life as it unfolds. You will find threads, whispers, and melodies about all these themes throughout this book. I live on the edge of psychological and spiritual constructs and I feel that these are embedded dimensions in all aspects of life. What is written here is not a manual but strongly suggests the importance of attending to the inner life of the educator in the service of living fully in the moment.

The following themes and ideas run through my writing, and I outline them here as guideposts for you. Educators need to

1. Be able to identify experientially and conceptually what is occurring in the moment in the classroom and within himself or herself, be able to derive some meaning from this, and be aware of his or her inner responses, as well as to be able to respond in ways that fit in both the inner and outer worlds of themselves and students.

2. Have the ability to see the process and describe it in process terms that leads to the identification of patterns. Noticing patterns is the basis for alchemy of the *prima materia* that is constituted by the classroom community, the individual students, and the curriculum content.

3. Have an evolved capacity to be accurately responsive in the moment to the other(s), self, and context, both locally and globally.

4. Distinguish behavior from the person who performs the behavior and develop abilities to see and connect with the person who initiates the behavior.

5. Have a developed capacity for awareness in the present that includes integration of thoughts, feelings, body sensation, other(s), relational experience, and what is called *spirit*.

6. Be aware of the influence of personal inner experiences on classroom events, and to have the ability to work with the personal and subjective inner and outer world experiences.
7. Be able to sense the emotions of others, identify emotions, and, on occasion, articulate them.
8. Focus on the heart of individuals and on the heart of the classroom community.
9. Know that acceptance does not preclude limits, responsibility, or even disliking.
10. Realize that community development is an underlying value, and to facilitate this development.
11. Be knowledgeable about the psychological dimension related to individuals, intersubjective, and group experience within the educational environment.
12. Be aware of the so-called external forces, such as family, peers, culture, and educational values and methods, that impinge on the educator, the learners, and the entire ethos of the educational environment.
13. Be attuned to the idea that there are unconscious forces at play that have a powerful influence on life in and out of classrooms.
14. Be sensitive and open to the possibility that there is something beyond the individual that lies within and behind all things and permeates a classroom.
15. Be aware of the soul's blueprint for each person, or at least that this is present.
16. Be conscious of the blueprint of the classroom community's soul.

Education needs to shift from the purely discursive and rational to *the heart of being* of individuals, groups, and all things. What do I mean by the heart of being? I do not mean only emotions. I do not mean just thoughts. I do not mean just physical reactions. I do not mean vague or even strongly felt intuitions on their own. I do mean an integrated sense of being, emotionally, intellectually, physically, and intuitively, that is responsive, reflective, and proactive in the world, that is reaching for a depth and breadth of meaning in a natural, therefore optimally energetic way (*wu-wei* in Daoism), and that seeks the source of all things.

PILOT LIGHTS: WHAT FIRES UP THE LIGHT ON THE PATH OF THIS INQUIRY

> True victory is not defeating an enemy. True victory gives love and changes the enemy's heart.
> —Morihei Ueshiba (O-Sensei), quote from Mitsugi Saotome
> (in Leonard, 2000, p. 150)

Surely, if as O-Sensei said, we might achieve victory by giving love to transform an enemy's heart; it makes eminent good sense to apply this transformational idea to classroom practice. A pilot light is a small flame that is always on and that serves as the initiatory spark for a bigger and hotter flame. O-Sensei has provided a pilot light.

Some years ago I had the opportunity to be at a day-long presentation with Dr. James Bugental, a white-haired elder who is one of the original developers of humanistic psychotherapy (see Bugental, 1992). He was 80 years old at the time and mounted the stage using two canes. His mind was sharp, his ideas clear and fascinating, and the demonstrations very engaging. What was particularly outstanding to me was how little he seemed to do during the demonstrations and yet how much happened. I asked him about the economy of his interventions, and he replied, "It's kind of like rolling a bicycle wheel along with a stick. It takes some effort to get it going, but once it's moving, it only requires the occasional tap to keep it going and on course." In my view education is like that. Educators need to be awake, put in sufficient effort at initiatory moments, have a feel for what is the optimal intervention in the moment and within the context, and the ability to stay with the process.

Here are 10 integrated pilot lights:

1. The ongoing discovery and inquiry into the purpose of a person's life and how to live well is core to all education. This discovery process is integrated with the adventure of the search for the source of all experience, along with the far reaches of its expression.

2. Apparently opposite conditions are part of a whole within a field and are a potentially generative and creative relationship.
3. Any given moment and set of experiences are part of a process. Everything is in motion.
4. Patterns are important. They lead to repetition and predictability. Some patterns are supportive, and others are wearing and destructive.
5. Aspects of the individual appear in the collective, and aspects of the collective appear in the individual.
6. Awareness is a critical dimension of life. It catalyzes change and growth. Lack of awareness has an opposite tendency.
7. Making meaning is central and requires a combination of thought and feeling. Thoughts without feeling are like dry bones, and feelings without thought are like a river over-running its banks. Humans have a propensity and a will to find or create meaning. Working toward integration of thought and feeling is ongoing even while accepting and valuing how things actually are at any given moment.
8. Humans have inner work potential, that is, a developed capacity for reflection on and work with personal inner experience. Inner work is an ongoing and central part of life, including professional life.
9. The depth and breadth of intimacy and connection that is possible, longed for, and needed by human beings is central to education, and it is incumbent on the educator to hold this vision.
10. The universe, both seen and unseen, is part of a field, within which there is interconnectedness.

THE GATELESS GATE

The great path has no gates,
Thousands of roads enter it.
When one passes through the gateless gate
He walks freely between heaven and earth.
—Mascetti (1996, p. 19)

The gateless gate for educators is present in their classrooms at almost every moment. It is really the barriers within themselves. Its presence is often signaled by an untenable event in the classroom. The way to freedom is through the gateless gate. The process of recognizing and engaging with the seeming difficulty and even impossibility of the gateless gate is a life-enhancing and life-engaging opportunity for educators and their students.

The Fine Line
On one side of the edge or another
Each person resides.

From one side everything is known
And taken for granted.

On the edge
Feelings are troubling, vision unclear.

On the far side
Another person emerges
And the unseen world
Is seen.
—a. cohen

ILLUSTRATION 1. *Over Sumatra.*

I Ching—Hexagram 49

No revolution in outer things is possible without prior revolution in one's inner way of being. Whatever change you aspire to in your affairs must be preceded by a change in heart, an active deepening and strengthening of your resolve to meet every event with equanimity, detachment, and innocent goodwill. When this spiritual poise is achieved within, magnificent things are possible without.

—B. B. Walker (1992)

References

Bugental, J. F. T. (1992). *The art of the psychotherapist: How to develop the skills that take psychotherapy beyond science*. New York: Norton.

Cohen, A., & Bai, H. (2006). Dao and Zen of teaching: Classroom as enlightenment field. *Educational Insights: On-Line Journal of the Center for Cross-faculty Inquiry in Education/the University of British Columbia, 11*(3). Retrieved on December 1, 2007, from the Educational Insights Web site: http://www.ccfi.educ.ubc.ca/publications/insights/v11n03/articles/bai/bai.html

Csikszentmihalyi, M. (1997). *Finding flow: The psychology of engagement with everyday life*. New York: Basic Books.

Leonard, G. (2000). *The way of aikido: Life lessons from an American sensei*. Toronto, ON, Canada: Penguin.

Mascetti, M. D. (Ed.). (1996). *Koans: The lessons of Zen*. New York: Hyperion.

Walker, B. B. (1992). *The I Ching or Book of Changes: A guide to life's turning points*. Retrieved on April 29, 2006, from http://www.elise.com/quotes/a/_ching_hexagram-49.phpReferences

CHAPTER 2

THE SHADOWY EDGES
OF THE PATH:
SHIFTING POWER
FROM THE TEACHER
TO THE STUDENTS

We will direct ourselves to: a type of inquiry that is critical, aware, and hopeful; and living contexts we find ourselves in every day. In so doing, we will quietly disrupt the surrounding social imaginary (there are multiple imaginaries in the world) by examining our senses our ability to imagine ourselves outside the social matrix. My hypothesis, albeit value loaded, is that the inquiries we perform...*as researchers,* practice an awareness of the intricate relationship between ourselves (an interpreter) and our research contexts (the living world).

—Meyer (2004)

The writing for this book has been a drama in my inner world about what matters to me in education and in life. Like my classrooms where

I give learners permission to be in all the ways that express who they are, I have given myself permission to speak freely from every place in me that I can access in the hope that I will speak to all those parts of you, the reader, that long to be noticed, reflected, spoken to, and joined with. I offer this as a potential way of healing and growing for human beings.

The following story from the Native American tradition was told to me by a Métis Medicine Man, Mechuskosees (personal communication, c. 1989):

> Fool's Crow had the ability to go inside a person's body to find out what was going on. A very sick young man came to him. Fool's Crow offered to go inside his body and look around. The young man agreed to this. Fool's Crow went inside his body and after a while he came out. He said, "You're going to die, but you will be alright." The young man spent several months with Fool's Crow and eventually he died peacefully.

A medicine man has the ability to find out what is wrong in the inner world. She or he does not give in to the pressures to conform to the everyday consciousness and pressures that are not consistent with a drum beat that is resonant with her or his soul and the soul of the universe. In this story, there is someone who is unwell. The medicine man and the one who is unwell meet and agree to investigate. From this inner work, it becomes clear that the young man will die and that healing will still be facilitated. Looking inside and being with the medicine man is endemic to the healing process. We humans need a sufficient number of healers to look "inside" to facilitate substantial and meaningful transformation in education.

My integrated engagement with life and studies has led to a series of ruminations and discoveries. In my many years of work as a psychotherapist where I see and feel the open psychic wounds of those who seek refuge in my office, I have had the realization that the educational system has contributed significantly, even decisively, to the wounding experience of my clients. My clients speak of alienation, feelings of despair, and loneliness. My students and colleagues also speak of these experiences. I have lived these experiences in my own life. My work as an educator of students who are studying for certificates or graduate degrees in counselling has been to look into the processes and structures that have contributed to these wounds and to provide an alternative and generative experience in an educational environment. At the foundation of my pedagogy is my own work on developing myself as a person. The widely revered wisdom in teaching circles is that we teach who we are (Palmer, 1998). I believe that this is so, and consequently, the most important qualification of being an educator is to work on ourselves in the service of feeling fully alive and becoming increasingly authentic[3] as an individual and in relationships. Before I go into talking about the educator's work, I wish to address the theme of wounding and education. I will use my own life as a case study and an illustration.

Peter Schellenbaum (1988/1990) says:

> I apply the term 'unloved' to people who at a critical point in their life—usually during childhood and adolescence—have had a traumatic experience with love, which penetrated their personality structure and now colours and influences all emotional relationships. (p. 13)

Schellenbaum goes on to talk about various ways in which this wounding manifests itself in individuals and relationships, including addictions, self-defeating behavior, personality traits that serve as defenses against emotions and intimacy, conflictual relationships, and so on.

My own experience of separation from myself and others was seeded early. I was raised mostly by my mother when I was an infant and young child. My father was in the Royal Canadian Air Force. World War II was taking place, and he was away serving his country. My mother was anxious about me, about him, and about life—understandably so. She was a young woman raising her two boys, in effect, as a single mom during wartime. Her attention to me was total but pervaded by her anxiety. Her fears contributed to an unconscious wound in the bond between us. As a result, I was compromised in my ability to feel secure within myself. This was further exacerbated by my father's emotional limitations when he did return. And then when I was 4, my brother was born. I was no longer number one. In fact, I was a very distant number two as the newcomer's needs and cuteness dominated my mother's attention. Another blow occurred 6 months later when we moved to Vancouver, which meant the loss of my very favorite and dear playmate, Vanda, along with my entire extended family. I became a withdrawn child who was viewed as unhappy and dissatisfied.

By the time I was sent off to grade 1, the wounding had taken a firm hold. Even though I was an able student, I was uncomfortable in school and shy with other children. I was fearful of being rejected and was socially awkward. As well, sitting still and learning by rote as I progressed through the grades contributed increasingly to a shutting down of my vitality along with my abilities to express myself. I was afraid of my teachers in a vague sort of way, and I was terrified of the principal because I knew that this role was invested with the authority and the right to strap me for certain misbehaviors. Even with the best of intentions on the part of my parents and my teachers, I was becoming a casualty of less than optimal child-rearing and educational practices. I was being systematically and persistently "taught" (by the "hidden curriculum") to be fearful of people, my emotions, and life even though the intent was to prepare me to live well. Fortunately, that is not the end of my story. Like the proverbial phoenix, I was destined, by my determination, to rise from the ashes.

My writing is not an autobiographical account of the process of my rebirth, although you will find some bits of this, but mostly it is a narrative of the outcomes as a result of extensive inner work to uncover my own wounds and allow the emergence of my more authentic self and its expression in my work as a psychotherapist and an educator. While individual stories will vary, I think that the pattern and themes of my experience regarding family and school relationships are not unusual. The shutting down of vitality and exuberance in children is tangible, and many elementary school teachers have suggested to me that by grade 4 the energy seems to have changed dramatically in most children. I think that school and schooling have a central role in this, and of course, educational institutions and practices are not separate from the society and culture within which they exist.

I must add that I believe that there is much more to life than healing wounds. I believe that there is within humans a powerful propensity to thrive, to move toward what draws them creatively, and to be moved by the life force that is within them. The same life force that assists in healing is also the life force that, when fully available, will allow the fullest and most whole expression of what is truly human. The clearing of that path and the facilitation of the fullest expression of the life force in students is what I believe education ought to be about. This writing is my effort to address the freeing of this force.

My own life has been a series of resistances to the worldly path of success. My resistance was not so much resistance per se as following another path—the path of "heart." Perhaps untypical is my drive and curiosity to look into myself and my experience to try and understand what was happening to me and to look for transformation in myself and my relationships. My propensity in this direction was fuelled by the drive to recover from my wounds, to be whole, and to express my creative potential in all dimensions of life. I will share more of my own process as illustration throughout the essays that follow.

I have always been moved by a strong desire to get to the heart of situations, relationships, and life. This drive has mostly, but not always, superseded any needs that I have for security and success in the world. In looking back, it seems that I have rather consistently walked with a different feeling, attitude, and intent than the majority of people. In the West, I believe that we are reaching the peak of consumerism; we are devouring our own nest and flesh. We are now the very goods and materials that we are devouring. The problem is that the consumption is incomplete. Listen to people who say "I need to look after myself, but first I have to get the job done." The label *Human Resources Department* names humans as resources. It is problematic enough to look at the world purely in instrumental terms and regard it as just another resource to consume. Seeing ourselves and others as resources to be consumed as well speaks to the degree of instrumentalism we face today. I am working on becoming less carnivorous toward myself and becoming more life loving and life giving for myself and hopefully for my students and clients.

RECOGNITION OF SOME EDUCATORS WHO CAME BEFORE

My ideas build on the efforts of many educators, scholars, and teachers of all kinds. What follows is a very brief description of the work of some selected humanistic writers and practitioners in the field of education who foreshadowed my work.

Harold C. Lyon, Jr. (1971) writes about the importance of emotions and also of education that addresses the whole person. He writes,

> Humanistic Education, the integration of cognitive learning with affective learning, is a natural outgrowth of Humanistic or Third Force psychology which has grown in large part as a reaction against the fact that the more academic psychologies (Behaviour-istic and Freudian) seem inadequate in dealing with the higher nature of humanness of man. (p. 3)

Lyon's emphasis on integration of intellect and feeling resonates in my work. I have gone further and discuss the importance of inter-subjective experience, inner experience, and the classroom as a deeply democratic community in development.

C. H. Patterson (1973) writes about self-actualization, feelings, and groups in education. He also writes about the humanistic teacher:

> Research indicates that good teachers and poor teachers cannot be differentiated on the basis of teaching 'methods.'...The method is inseparable from the person of the teacher; in fact, the person of the teacher is more important than the method. (p. 97)

I am in agreement with Patterson. He describes the characteristics of good teachers and how this translates into praxis. Excellent teachers are aware of their own inner experiences and perform various kinds of inner work with these experiences in the service of developing their authentic-ity and abilities.

George Leonard (1969) writes about the need for education to foster and encourage experience and how "Education, at best, is ecstatic"

(p. 16). This seems to be a radical difference from what occurs in many classrooms where drudgery and boredom seem to be the norm. He asks: Schools for what?

- To learn the commonly agreed-upon skills and knowledge of the ongoing culture… to learn it joyfully… .
- To learn how to ring creative changes on all that is currently agreed upon.
- To learn delight, not aggression; sharing, not eager acquisition; uniqueness, not narrow competition.
- To learn heightened awareness… increased empathy for other people (a new kind of citizenship education).
- To learn how to enter and enjoy varying states of consciousness, in preparation for a life of change.
- To learn how to explore and enjoy the infinite possibilities in relations between people… .
- To learn how to learn. (pp. 132–133)

Leonard's response to the question about what schools are for rang the bell of change.

A. S. Neill (1960) developed a school for children that ran on principles of democracy and the belief that with appropriate structure, encouragement, and freedom within carefully designed limits, children would do what was in their best interests and would recover their curiosity and joy for learning. He wrote, "I hold that the aim of life is to find happiness, which means to find interest. Education should be a preparation for life" (p. 24).

Indeed, education is life, and educational environments and educators ought to try to draw out happiness.

I will highlight just one aspect of Carl Rogers' (1980) views about education. He says:

> A facilitative learning environment is provided. In meetings of the class or of the school as a whole, an atmosphere of realness,

of caring, and of understanding listening is evident. This climate may spring initially from the person who is the perceived leader. As the learning process continues, it is more and more often provided by the learners for one another. (p. 300)

This quote highlights several important themes. The process of shifting power from the teacher to the students, with facilitation as central, will potentially alter the views of students about learning and about education, and the approach contests traditional models of education and learning.

I have only offered a few brief morsels from some educators who were interested in the human dimension and humanistic education. Their ideas were radical at the time. Interestingly, these ideas are still radical. I think this is so for a couple of reasons. First, these seem to be emotionally conservative times and the riskiness of such an approach is threatening for individuals, institutions, and the overall status quo. Secondly, some of the original humanistic educators could be best described as naïve. Their attempts to write about their experience were often vague and strange even to sympathetic ears. As well, the efforts of some to emulate what they thought was good practice turned out not to be good practice and, at times, led to situations that were chaotic, not good for leaning, and, at times, just unsafe. My writing is aimed at learning from and building on the past.

The Promise of Education for Living Well

Part of the unspoken promise of education currently is that those who are successfully educated will have the most resources and the best chance for survival and living well. This is at odds with my idea of living well. The survival orientation itself is problematic. It promotes competition and a lack of care for others and the planet, and negates thriving by failing to address it or mention it. Positioning on either side of the polarity is problematic. Both survival and thriving are very human. The crucial distinction is the development of consciousness that can see the possibilities in both sides of apparently opposing positions and is skillful in recognizing the edges that these dichotomies represent, is able to metacommunicate about them, and is able and willing to provide facilitation to bring out the message of both and support the potential integration that may be attempting to emerge. While the meaning of success needs to be redefined, uncritical derision of those who are successful in material ways is also problematic. Many of these prosperous people are the leaders in creating the institutions that will further the nurturance of healers, lovers, artists, poets, educators, and others. Refocusing the idea of success to mean being a humane human being, with material success being seen as a potential accompaniment to this human beingness, seems to be a worthy undertaking. We need to work to develop the consciousness that can see both sides of polarized positions inclusively.

In my late teens, it occurred to me that freedom in a market-driven democracy depended on being financially independent. It seemed clear to my teenage self that without adequate financial resources, I would be subject to the will and whim of others and that my life would be more of a burden and liability that I would have to bear than an exhilarating and exuberant adventure. I recall when I was about 14 telling my mother that I was bored. I was typical in my statement, but something else was happening. I had a vague inner glimmering of the culture and my place within it, and I didn't like what I saw. She responded, "You're just like your father. You expect everything to be fun. You'll see that life is not always interesting. Most of life *is* boring. That's just how it is." In retrospect, I realize that she wanted to protect me from the pain of the mundane aspects of her life and that she believed was the nature of life. I distinctly remember my very powerful and pervasive thought at that moment, "Not for me. My life will not be that way." And, it has not been that way. At that point, I lacked the experience to appreciate the inner commitment that I was making—to move toward a personally meaningful life. Consonant with my age and the culture, I was thinking much more in terms of fun, excitement, and adventure. So, even though Dr. Seuss (1990) was not on my radar screen, his words fit my consciousness at that time:

> Today is your day.
> You're off to Great Places!
> You're off and away!
>   ....

You're on your own. And you know what you know.
And YOU are the guy who'll decide where to go. (pp. 1–2)

Many years later, after living through my full share of pain and loss, grief and joy, success and failure, I look back and see that there is no way I could have planned the life I have led. Leonard Cohen, cited in an interview originally published in the *Globe and Mail* and reproduced online (Saunders, 2001), states,

> Everybody eventually comes to the conclusion that things are not unfolding exactly the way they wanted, and that the whole enterprise has a basis that you can't penetrate. Nevertheless, you live your life as if it's real. But with the understanding: It's only a thousand kisses deep, that is, with that deep intuitive understanding that this is unfolding according to a pattern that you simply cannot discern.

I am not sure what I had planned. I am pretty sure that I was brought up to be a regular person. It did not work. The difficulties that life offered became catalysts for growth and development, personally and professionally. As it turns out, I have seen some great places, many days have been "mine," and some have not. I have become increasingly better at not interfering with what seems to be natural as it unfolds. I have some regrets—but not too many. They weigh me down occasionally but not too often. I hope that the "great places," within you that are a "thousand kisses deep" will show up as you read what is contained on these pages.

WORK FOR WHAT?

I viewed work as a compulsory and coercive activity that everybody did because they had to and which, for the most part, they did not want to do. I formulated the view that work as it seemed to be constituted would require too many hours away from my real interests, whatever they might be. The idea of meaningful work that is conducted humanely and is materially productive seems to be an idea that is not even on the horizon for most. Essentially, my ideas on this have developed from this original foundation and have only been enhanced by what I have experienced and witnessed. The amount of discussion about work stress; work days lost due to health failures, alcohol and substance abuse; and increasing injury rates at work all bear witness to this idea that human beings are breaking down under the load (Fiorini, 2007). Education has the possibility of fostering an alternative dream that values the humans who work in the service of or toward the well-being of themselves and the society and is sensitive to their needs and vulnerabilities. I hope that changes as I am outlining provide some sense of alternatives and possibilities.

Another propensity in the world, including the field of education, is to blame and pathologize individuals who stand out, those who are considered failures, and perhaps surprisingly, those who are deemed successes (Cohen, 1996). In many areas and professions, including psychology and education, within the culture there is this blaming and pathologizing predisposition. The whole system of diagnosis of disorders has a propensity to ensure that unhappy and undesired ways of being actually continue. How does that work? The blamed and pathologized feel disempowered, and then instead of seeking ways to become empowered within themselves, they become jealous, envious, or even hateful. Worse, in my view, are the occasions when the identified "patient" or "poor student" aligns with the "diagnoses" and sees themselves as "sick," "incapable," or, at times, uses the diagnosis as a justification and rationale for their inability to function in the ways to which they aspire. The alternative described here is to identify what is actually happening, what potential is buried within the limitations that show up, what factors are at work within the individual from their personal history, and what systemic and structural issues are reinforcing a nonrewarding experience. Forces conspire within individuals beyond their conscious intent to create personalities, beliefs, and behavior that are other than what might emerge if the environment was nurturing and encouraging. The focus on achievement at the expense of developing humane ways of being is costly to the person who demonstrates such ways and to those around him or her. As John Taylor Gatto (1999) writes:

> There must be some reason we are called human *beings* and not human *doings*. And I think this reason is to commemorate the way we can make the best of our limited time by alternating effort with reflection, and reflection completely free of the get-something motive. Whenever I see a kid daydreaming in school, I'm careful never to shock the reverie out of existence. (p. 170)

Gatto suggests here, strongly, that there is more to life than checking off an endless list of to-do's, and that we ought not to shock "reverie out of existence." Such shock negates the existence of those who are in a reverie state. A consistent pattern of such shock translates into a felt sense of being unloved and unwanted. This pattern of shock can lead to the development of a personality structure and ways of being that allow the person to survive, but not to thrive, and disrupts the capacity to live authentically (Miller, 1987/2005; Schellenbaum, 1988/1990). Such persons may develop a great facility to compete and will be noted as *winners* within the competitive context of the world, but these people often are unhappy, unable to live authentically, and are not able to experience "interbeing" (Hanh, 1975) with the whole cosmos including fellow humans. Authenticity in a person or persons is a way of being that is the enactment of a depth and breadth of feeling integrated with body awareness, movement, thought, connection to personal and collective history, cultural myths, and spirit. What you will find as you read through the pages that follow are ideas and practices that point toward a more authentic possibility of being as individuals, in relationship, and in community. Individuals are tiny representations of an entire culture and the world, and the world is an immense representation of an individual. From a life-myth perspective, their shortcomings, limits, and deficits are clusters of experience that contain the seeds for what is trying to happen and what an individual is *trying* to become and express. People have been given a certain set of experiences that constitute their work for this life, and the possibility he or she is given is to perform this work and clear the way for the more authentic experience to happen. Put another way, it is perhaps better to say that *it* is trying to happen and the learning is about how to allow emergence and becoming.

N/o/ne is More
No chicken,
No egg,
No flesh,
No bones,

No Nothing.
——a. cohen

REFERENCES

Cohen, A. (1996). *One year process-directed counselling training manual.* Vancouver, BC: Life Force Publications.

Fiorini, K. (2007). *Work-life balance and well-being in public practice accounting.* Unpublished master's thesis, Royal Roads University, Victoria, BC, Canada.

Gatto, J. L. (1999). Education and the western spiritual tradition. In S. Glazer (Ed.), *The heart of learning: Spirituality in education* (pp. 151–171). New York: Jeremy P. Tarcher/Putnam.

Hahn, T. N. (1975). *The miracle of mindfulness* (M. Ho, Trans.). Boston: Beacon.

Leonard, G. B. (1969). *Education and ecstasy.* New York: Delta.

Lyon Jr., H. C. (1971). *Learning to feel-feeling to learn: Humanistic education for the whole man.* Columbus, OH: Charles E. Merril.

Meyer, K. (2004). *Syllabus EDCI 565B: Living Inquiry.* Unpublished manuscript, University of British Columbia, Vancouver, Canada.

Miller, A. (2005). *The drama of being a child: The search for the true self.* New York: Harper & Rowe. (Original work published 1987)

Neill, A. S. (1960). *Summerhill: A radical approach to child rearing.* New York: Hart.

Palmer, P. (1998). *The courage to teach: Exploring the inner landscape of a teacher's life.* San Francisco: John Wiley & Sons.

Patterson, C. H. (1973). *Humanistic education.* Englewood Cliffs, NJ: Prentice-Hall.

Rogers, C. (1980). *A way of being.* New York: Houghton Mifflin.

Saunders, D. (2001, September 1). State of grace. *Toronto Globe and Mail*. Retrieved on October 13, 2008, from http://www.webheights.net/10newsongs/press/globe.htm

Schellenbaum, P. (1990). *The wound of the unloved: Releasing the life energy* (T. Nevill, Trans.). Dorset, U.K.: Element Books. (Original work published 1988)

Seuss. (1990). *Oh, the places you'll go!* Toronto, ON, Canada: Random House.

CHAPTER 3

WE TEACH
WHO WE ARE
AND THAT IS THE PROBLEM

The Master in the art of living makes little distinction between his work and his play, his labor and his leisure, his mind and his body, his education and his recreation, his love and his religion. He hardly knows which is which. He simply pursues his vision of excellence in whatever he does, leaving others to decide whether he is working or playing. To him he is always doing both.

—Zen Buddhist Text[4]

Why are some teachers effective and influential and able to contribute to the development of the human dimension, while others are not? There is very often a gap between how teachers present themselves to students and what they are actually experiencing within; this gap is costly to students in terms of learning curriculum and about being human. It is also costly to the educator as it precipitates "burnout" and compromises their inner world and their felt sense of integrity and wholeness. As the gap widens, effectiveness diminishes further, and conversely, as congruence and authenticity increase, effectiveness increases. By *effectiveness*, I am referring to the teacher's capacity to engage with students personally, have students engage with each other personally, develop a sense of aliveness and community in the classroom, and have the students engage energetically with curriculum material.

In the current literature on teacher formation and development, the closest I have found to this idea is in the work of Parker Palmer (1990; 1998). However, even Palmer falls short. He does not offer detailed descriptions about how educators can practically move towards becoming more exemplary educators. Palmer shares many appealing ideas and stories but with little indication as to how the reader could develop their own abilities to perform similar classroom miracles. This essay offers the view that a significant part of the success of these phenomenal educators is connected to the self-knowledge gained from *attention to and work with their inner* life that allows them to have advanced ability to be fully present in the moment. I describe inner experience and inner work—specifically the relationship between metaskill development, authenticity, and presence—and I try to make the case for its importance for educators.

THE COST OF THE GAP

Many educators struggle with issues such as curriculum and its delivery, class size, student diversity, demands for inclusive education, systemic indifference, professional expectations that conflict with personal needs, lack of collegial connection and support, lack of quality supervision, loss of passion for learning, subject matter in conflict with student indifference, and a focus on grades. They complain to their colleagues, partners, spouses, family, and friends. They blame themselves. They worry. They get sick. They burn out and up. They try harder. They use substances, distractions, and a form of willpower that overcomes and disenfranchises their own genuine needs. They work in isolation and feel overwhelmed. Many hours are devoted to attempting to make it all work. Sometimes they even succeed. Many comments and criticisms could be made about the system, supervision, teacher, and education, but my purpose here is to introduce the background to the gap.

A study (Talmor, Seiter & Feigin, 2005) related burnout to a lack of inclusion, having numbers of students with special needs at more than 20% of classroom population, organizational factors, psychological factors, and low levels of social support. While each of these areas is worthy of investigation on its own, I will centralize the inner world of the educator here. Her or his inner world is core to areas where the teacher could exercise more personal agency. I am not diminishing the importance of the very real issues in classrooms nor do I dispute that changes in those areas would be helpful, but the point that I want to make is that there is always a personal and inner dimension associated with classroom experience. I believe that work on these dimensions will lead to a better classroom experience for educators and their students, and a lack of work on these will lead inexorably back to the original difficulty. Here is an example of an imaginary classroom experience with older teenaged boys and how inner awareness and work are helpful:

> A female educator is working with a class that has a number of male students who she finds attractive. She finds herself fantasizing about relationships and sexual possibilities with some of these students. She comes to class full of guilt, shame, and worry that somehow her imagined liaisons will come to light and jeopardize her job. She realizes that, as a result, she is actually avoiding engaging with these students, and consequently, they are getting less attention personally and academically. She engages in inner work that helps her to see that she is, indeed, relating to her own fantasies and that the men are serving as scaffolding for these imaginings. The result of her inner work is that her practice changes. She is able to see the young men much more accurately, nurture a proper relationship with them, and lessen her own burnout potential by dealing with her internalized stress and being able to come to class in a more relaxed state.

In this particular case, while unlikely to happen, presumably the teacher's problem could have been solved by moving the young men she found attractive out of the class. However, this would not have resolved her core issue, which certainly would have recurred at another time. A more likely example for exclusion might be where an educator has issues with aggressive males. It is not hard to imagine a request for assessment, along with many examples of behavior deemed to be inappropriate. The males might then be referred for counseling, psychiatric assessment, or moved to a different class with a different teacher, or a combination of these measures. All this will appear to help the teacher, help the students, and alleviate the problem. However, my contention is that in many of these situations, the situation could and would be resolved within the classroom to everyone's benefit if the teacher was able to resolve their own inner experience of fear.

To be clear, I am not offering inner work as a panacea for the isolation that many teachers experience. I am suggesting it can be helpful, and in fact, I am making the case that it needs to be central to any practice of education. Ideally, the ideas and practices contained here would be integrated with systemic support. However, in current educational environments, this is often not the case, and the systemic challenges are many and complex. Educators can learn about the process of inner work by consulting with someone who is already skilled in this practice by reading widely about counseling and meditation methods; reading philosophical, spiritual, and religious texts; and through their own unique creative inquiry. Elements that can be addressed through inner work are personal, relational, transpersonal, and spiritual.

In the following sections, I offer a number of ideas associated with my core thesis about inner work:

1. Familiarity with and ability to access inner experience contributes to an authenticity that is compelling and appealing for students.
2. Educators can perform some form of inner work that is interactive with and responsive to their outer experiences.
3. Inner work can lead to transformation into new ways of being and a changed sense of identity that influences practice and invites new responses from learners, which can recursively precipitate further inner work.

4. Inner work is germane to the development and nurturance of fully alive metaskills[5] in the human dimensions of curiosity, warmth, excitement, and compassion, to name a few.

The contact with and the capacity to use consciously an exceptional depth and range of metaskills sets apart those educators whom students want to be with and those to whom they are less attracted. These educators are perceived as authentic[6] in their way of being.

INNER WORK AND INNER LIFE

The term *inner work* refers to reflective practices conducted under the gaze of consciousness, which depends on a developed capacity to self-observe, to witness experience. This type of awareness is not something teacher education addresses nor is it a part of the culture that most of us inhabit, yet it is the crucial and central key to personal inner work that will facilitate the narrowing of the previously mentioned gap between outer presentation of self and inner experience. Inner work is a way of working on and with perceptions, sensations, memories, and cognitions, all of which constitute a person's experience. Inner life consists of inner awareness and inner reflections on thoughts, feelings, images, dreams, reactions, ruminations, and processes that can be either internally generated or generated in response to an external event. Central to these ideas is that there are internal, private processes occurring all the time within educators in response to experiences, both internal and external, and that these internal experiences are recognizable by that person.

Within Western culture, the separation between inner and outer life and the privileging of the outer world over the inner world seems to be an accepted and largely unconscious decision. Emphasis on grades, test scores, and intellectual achievement in educational environments with no acknowledgment of the emotional or physical life of students is a prime example. This separation has become so embedded in consciousness that few seem to notice that their lives have become an unending series of tasks. The idea of taking time for reflection, stopping and actually attending to experience as it is unfolding instant by instant and attending to life as it is now, is not even deemed worthy of the time it would take to declare the project unworthy. The education system and the mainstream culture within which I grew up quietly and perniciously insinuated a separation between inner and outer experience and this has indeed caused me and multitudes of others difficulties. A similar but different distinction that has a relationship to this inner and outer dualism is the mind-body disruption, which is a common experience in Western cultures (Murphy, 1993). I believe that the process of reconnecting these domains is restorative for individuals and particularly important for educators.

Not only do we separate the inner and the outer but also we privilege the outer over and above the inner. In our culture, we look up to those who are "movers and shakers," who are the "winners" in the competition for status, money, possessions, and being "beautiful," but we speak dismissively of those who are extensively involved in inner work. Predispositions to perform inner work are derided as "touchy-feely," "soft headed," "navel gazing," "time wasting," and on and on. There is little guide and guidance for us to engage in inner work. Here is an example from my own experience. At an early point in my career, I was the unit supervisor of a residential treatment unit for severely disturbed male and female adolescents. The unit was one of three similarly configured ones. As an outcome of my own inner work and my belief that it was important to individuals, communities, and organizations, I designed the structure of the unit to put inner work for the staff in the foreground in combination with a strong and direct focus on the interpersonal relationships and communication between the staff. This was not practiced in the other two units. There was a relentless supply of comments from staff and supervisors from the other units, including how much time we wasted on staff's personal problems and how much navel-gazing we did. Consistently overlooked were specific quantifiable phenomena. Our unit had one third of the staff sick time, much less staff turnover, virtually no staff time lost due to injury, and a significantly lower incidence of critical incidents with our residents.

In the service of healing myself and accessing my potential, I have learned to observe my own inner experiences and to work with these experiences, and in classroom and organizational contexts I have helped others to learn this practice as well. I have had help with this, and I have also developed skills on my own.

E. F. Schumacher, author of the seminal work in ecology that became a modern day classic, *Small Is Beautiful: Economics as if People Mattered* (1973/1999), came to the discovery of inner work and its power rather late in his life. Inner work was not likely part of his school curriculum. In his autobiographical work, *This I Believe and Other Essays* (1997), he talks about his revelatory experience on being advised "that I could greatly improve my health and happiness by devoting fifteen minutes a day to certain relaxation and concentration exercises—which were explained to me" (p. 215). He goes on, "My way of living had never allowed me to discover those inward parts let alone to notice what had been put into them." He then speaks about what he considers to be most important: "This inner organ with its indwelling spirit of Truth is really the most wonderful thing. It tells me whether something is Truth—the truth that shall make us free—sometimes long before my reason is able to understand how it *could* be such" (p. 216).

WHO ARE THE INNER WORKERS AND WHAT HAPPENS IN THEIR CONSCIOUSNESS?

Schumacher describes succinctly the life-changing effect of this discovery of his inner life. That which was previously words now divulges its true meaning. He says that while this *truth* may be uncomfortable, it does lead us to the critical question in life, "distinguishing the True from the False with regard to the only question which we cannot sidestep, about which we cannot be agnostic—the question of what to do with our lives" (p. 217).

This question is important for any human being, and its relevance for educators is surely apparent, both for educators and for their students. This question is in the atmosphere on a daily basis in classrooms.

An educator who is addressing this question on a consistent basis through inner work surely will model for students a way of being that will serve the process of education in a profound way. I believe and am arguing that not attending to the inner life will have an opposite and negative effect on the educator and learners.

I identify myself as an inner worker. I have found my motivations for this process to be similar to others whom I have encountered in my personal and professional life. Inner workers are spiritual pilgrims that Jack Miller (1988) describes as "people who have awakened to their true identities and manifest this awakening in their lives and work. They work and live their lives in a place of love and compassion as they are not trying to meet the never ending demands of the ego. At the same time they have retained their humanity; they are not hermits or unreachable saints." (p. 2)

Miller is describing people who are in a process of awakening and who demonstrate this by their way of being, and not by any particular action. He describes some characteristics of such individuals:

> Firstly, they have the courage to confront many of our traditional approaches to healing and spirituality. In many cases they have been pathfinders....

> The re-evaluation of traditional structures is part of the pilgrim's role....

> Another characteristic of these individuals is the depth and authenticity of their work. Their realness has a powerful impact on others....

> ...the Pilgrims see the world as a "school" for learning and understanding who we really are rather than a place to be exploited and manipulated. When the Pilgrims have confronted suffering in their own life, they have not pushed it away, but viewed the pain as a vehicle for spiritual growth....

> ...they have not cultivated disciples or followers, but instead have encouraged people to do their own work (e.g., meditation) and trust their own heart as a guide....

> ...the centrality of love and forgiveness. (pp. 2–4)

Miller outlines core characteristics of inner workers, that is, people who are motivated to learn about life, whose approach to others tends to selflessness, are swimming at the edge or beyond of the cultural stream, have chosen to move to alternate locations and seek that which is not easily found, and who want to help others to realize their human potential.

A major part of the difficulty of undertaking inner work is that, unlike what the terminology might suggest, it is not something that comes naturally and easily, like sitting down and having a cup of tea or talking to a friend. An essential ingredient of inner work is the development of witness consciousness.[7] Other names for this are the observer-self, intuition, Hara, or more recently, metacommunicator (Arnold Mindell, 1990/1991). Using Arnold Mindell's vocabulary, the metacommunicator notices what is happening and comments without judgment. Things are accepted as they are in the moment and neither liking, nor not liking, is implied. The metacommunicator participates in the exquisite interaction between inner and outer experience. The metacommunicator is the aspect of personal consciousness that has the capacity for awareness and is a crucial aspect of an educator who facilitates exceptional pedagogical experience. But how does the metacommunicator develop? Arnold Mindell (1990/1991) writes, "There is a sort of 'fair observer,' a metacommunicator who, when she or he is awake, can observe…as if from above, on the mountain top, and is able to talk about these insights and perceptions" (p.19). He continues,

> If you are identified with only one part of yourself, then there is no metacommunicator, no one is there to work with this part. You cannot decide to investigate it further, to amplify it, or even to amplify the suffering because you are it. One of the reasons for working on yourself is to develop a relationship to and between different aspects of yourself and to allow these inner roles and relationships to unfold.
>
> The more you work on yourself, the less you will identify with only one part, and the more you will metacommunicate. Thus even if you are submerged in some difficult piece of fate, you…can go deeper into the message and story of suffering. (p. 85)

An increasing capacity to hold differing positions and perspectives in consciousness is indicative of the metacommunicator at work and is an integral dimension of any quest for authenticity. A well-developed meta-communicator is the part of consciousness that makes it possible for the educator to shift fluidly between a multiplicity of roles and perspectives and to monitor feedback that indicates the need for shifts in states of consciousness and roles. The metacommunicator mediates between inner and outer experience and both facilitates and develops as an outcome of conscious attention to experiences. This level of awareness gets the educator out of the intrinsic trap of positioning and provides opportunity to facilitate between positions. This supports processes of integration and heightened awareness. By having a metaposition from which to observe experience, the educator is freed up to take a position consciously, take on an apparently opposing position, comprehend holistically whatever values are present and embodied in those positions, and creatively facilitate dialogue between the positions. This inner work can be done with inner differences and conflicts.[8]

WHY IS INNER WORK
ESPECIALLY IMPORTANT TO EDUCATORS?

Educators carry an inordinate amount of power and influence in relation to students within learning contexts. If they are unaware of how they use this power, it is very likely to be misused. As well, if educators are unaware of what is happening inside of them that affects their way of being in the classroom, then they are likely to, at best, create a numbing and dull atmosphere and, at worst, they will increase the scope of the wounds that already exist within classroom community members. On the other side, if educators are aware and growing by way of their own inner work, they will model aliveness and offer a classroom opportunity that is full of excitement and curiosity.

Specifically, if an educator assumes a dominant position, which can be an inevitable outcome of insufficient acknowledgment and integration of inner experience, then the timespirit[9] of the leader freezes, and consequently, any leadership function or initiative that might emerge from students will be suppressed. A *timespirit* is an evolved form of the concept of role. It is a role that emerges at a particular time and place. It can be "held" by a person, disowned, or just be in the atmosphere waiting to come into play. An educator who does not have consciousness that is in a process of intentional development is unknowingly dominated by the effects of unconscious forces that are inevitably oppressive to him or her and learners. Even if the educator's unconscious is dictating what seems right by the norms of the community, something will still seem to be wrong. What is wrong is that the unconscious process will show up in an incongruity of expression because of the unrecognized internal conflict. Learners will be detrimentally affected as they will hear the overt message and pick up, probably without realizing it, the secondary and conflicting message.

By nature of his or her position, the educator does have a sanctioned dominance. The effect of inner work is to ensure that this dominance is used judiciously and appropriately. An outcome of failure to acknowledge inner experience can manifest as the misuse of rank (Fuller, 2003), that is, the use of rank to further personal agendas, whether conscious or unconscious. I hasten to add that the sanctioned dominant position is often unwisely thrown out under the misguided view that the position itself is a problem when the issue is really improper use of the position, role, and rank. Acts of unconscious suppression of students also have the effect of suppressing the leader. Arnold Mindell states succinctly, "There are no permanent roles. Anyone can be in any role. At the same time the roles themselves are in flux" (1995, p. 42). For example, it could be the case that the part of the leader that is relaxed and receptive—that is also a learner and just another member of the educational community—is suppressed because the leader is held by the notion that he or she must be "in charge" and seem to be knowledgeable about everything. Inner work is the pathway to the authentic self, the liberation of creative energies, and the protection against misuse of power and authority.

IN THE PRESENCE OF AN INNER WORKER

A further meaning of presence is *in the presence of*. Somehow the presence of the human who educates imbues the space with something ineffable. There is something about bearing, manner, style, way of being, and beingness itself that is significant. The idea might better be conveyed by reference to melody, poetry, rhythm, or metaphor. The leader conveys something that goes beyond the words—the construction of the words into sentences, the sentences into paragraphs, the paragraphs into sections, and the sections into an entire textual production. The students may have a sense of something deeper that inspires a leader. What is this thing?

Hafiz (in Ladinsky, 1999, p. 99) asks:

How Do I Listen?

How
Do I
Listen to others?
As if everyone were my Master
Speaking to me
His
Cherished
Last
Words.

Is there not a sense of being in love conveyed by these few words? Not being in love as in love with another but literally being contained within an atmosphere, a field, that is constituted by love and that permeates all that is within it. Love is simultaneously a noun and a verb. Is not true presence synonymous with love?

I believe that presence is equivalent to love. Giving full presence to another is, I believe, the greatest gift a person can offer. Another way of saying this is to equate presence with full attention. For example, without such presence, there is no empathy, only sympathy or pity. This latter, at times, indicates an objectification of the other and is not the same as full recognition. I believe the concepts of empathy and identification are often confused. Empathy is the ability to feel another's experience. It is not pity or sympathy. Demonstrations of empathy indicate that a person has proceeded in their developmental process past the level of only knowing self-as-central. To feel empathy does not mean to be totally identified with the other's experience and become lost in the feelings. It means being sufficiently present for the experience to know it while maintaining a consciousness and a presence that is able to observe the experience and comment on it while not being completely consumed by emotions.

Learners are inspired by the modeling of a teacher who personifies change and growth—someone who emanates aliveness, a curiosity about life, a willingness to take risks, interconnectedness, and who demonstrates self-awareness. A teacher who is not able to be present in a substantial and meaningful way will not be able to demonstrate these qualities, which are integrally related. It is incongruous if an educator teaches for change of thinking while simultaneously demonstrating little interest in him or herself, others, and personal change. In educational environments the damage accrues to learners, who tend to shut down in the presence of unconsciously conflicted role models, who are already damaged and numbed to the effects on themselves and others.

The work of addressing the inner experience for an educator is in the service of recognizing the "interareness" of the educator and the educational community that includes the environment, the atmosphere, the educational leader, and the learners. The educator's task is to recognize interbeing. How does this happen in the educator? How are the educator and the milieu parts of one whole? The educator's presence is core to these ways of being.

INNER WORK PRIMER

What constitutes the activity called inner work? What kinds of "things" do inner workers do? What is their essential method, if there is any? For example, how do inner workers develop the aforementioned metacommunicator?

Inner workers require ongoing development of personal awareness, including

1. Observing experience while being engaged.
2. Reflecting through memory after the initial experience is past.
3. Imagining possibilities.
4. Staying focused on inner experience.
5. Employing a variety of methods and perceptual frameworks that allow and facilitate inner work.

All of these abilities are associated with the capacity to manifest, live in, and work with nonordinary states of consciousness. The states themselves are not the goal. They are evidence that usual consensus reality has, at least, temporarily moved into the background. These nonordinary states are the ground from which inner experience and the doors of perception open. The ordinary states have their uses. They are the states within which I look after everyday things. I remember my appointments, brush my teeth, call my friend, buy groceries, and so on. The nonordinary states allow seeing life, self, relationship, other(s), and the nonhuman world as part of a collective whole. Consciousness shifts. Conflicts and differences are seen as part of a whole. Roles are seen as separate from the person. Social reality becomes a construction rather than a fixed reality. My identity is experienced as not fixed. This nonordinary consciousness is a living and lived experience. It is felt emotionally and physically and leads to a deeper understanding of self and life. Possibilities for unique creative expression are freed up, aspects of which for long-forgotten reasons have been blocked from awareness and expression.

Certain inner experiences attract the attention of the inner worker and send a signal for attention. This signal can take the form of excesses or cessations, emotional responses, symptoms, dreams, relationship problems, and behavioral shifts. These experiences are frequently connected to personal history. Often central to this unfolding is identifying the inner opposition (IO) that prevents this emergence. The IO is embedded within a person and is working against what a deeper part of that person wants and that is trying to emerge. This IO very often has a good intent, but this good intent is no longer attached to anything that is actually present. It is a perpetuation of the response that made sense in the original pattern of experience. Finding out what message is being expressed by both the deeper self and the IO, and establishing a relationship between them, facilitates what is trying to happen and is an important aspect of inner work. These internal difficulties are reflective of outer difficulties. Identifying inner experiences implies the possibility of working with them in ways that involve some form of self-reflection. The forms can include counseling or psychotherapy, meditation, journal writing, peer support, mentoring, supervision, and any personally meaningful relationship. The methods used can involve relating experiences to any, all, or some of personal history, day and night dreams, personality structures, behavior, symptoms, relationship issues, group issues, the world, and states of consciousness.

Here is an example of what inner workers do that might be deemed unusual. They take the stance that the ominous outer world and dream events, objects, and figures hold the key to deeper understandings about themselves and life and that not dealing with these is a guarantee of repetition. Alfried Längle (ECPS Colloquium, University of British Columbia, February 3, 2005) attributed the following to Viktor Frankl, "I take everything as a question to myself." Inner workers have this approach and use these questions to investigate the deepest meanings of difficult pieces of fate. Inner workers are in the process of exploring all aspects of their lives by entering intentionally into those areas that call for inquiry and by dealing with fears, feelings, and experiences of not-knowing. Developing an openness of heart and mind is both experience and process for inner workers.

Through inner work, people can learn to value difficult experiences as much as pleasant ones and are learning endlessly about the potential contained in both kinds of experiences. Further, there is an awareness of the continuum between the extremes of dark and light and that the depth and breadth of all experience is worthy of exploration. The capacity to live in states of not-knowing and in and with ambiguity is important to the inner worker. There is an awareness that life is changing constantly and that the capacity to be conscious with this change and process is an ever-evolving challenge.

INNER WORK SAMPLER: MY OWN AND OTHER'S

The following narrative is a description of an experience that I had. I have written in the present tense to make the experience as alive as possible within this textual form:

> I am sitting in a meeting with a group of fellow graduate students. An educational leader with a role that legitimates a dominant position is taking up most of the time allocated for discussion. This is a recurrent experience. I along with my colleagues in our lesser roles are sitting submissively and allowing the monologue to go on and on. I feel very frustrated and am doodling and thinking about other things. Suddenly I remember that this is a familiar situation not only here but also in other circumstances in my life. I remember my father and his tendency to dominate conversations and the very similar feelings that I had while with him. I reflect on this and then slowly bring my awareness back to the meeting. I begin to observe the leader who is dominant and my colleagues who are submissive. I become keenly curious about what is actually happening with each person, at least what is observable and what is going on between people. I observe various clues that my colleagues are drifting in and out of attending. I begin to see signs of anxiety in the leader and imagine that there is a positive intent to get things deemed to be important across to us. My curiosity increases. I wonder to myself, 'What is going on? What can I do?' My feeling changes from dullness and frustration to a feeling of enhanced curiosity, compassion, care, and empowerment. I keep looking for openings. I keep coming up against my own fears. I do not have much of a personal relationship with this person. I can not find a way in. This person is drowning and taking the group down with her. There is nothing in the culture of this little community that allowed any intervention that I could imagine. I feel my body relaxing. I am beginning to come to terms with my own helplessness and my sense of self-preservation that suggests that I should take the least worst option, namely, be relaxed, alert for opportunity, and otherwise mostly quiet. What I can offer the situation is my compassionate and quiet attention.

The idea and experience of looking and wondering is a huge shift and a felt experience of having my feelings that have been closed off become available. I have found a better way to be in this situation. I am now more likely to be helpful if opportunity arose, and at the least, I was less likely to be a contributor to worsening the situation.

What my experience demonstrates is a move out of one level of reality into another. Initially, I was able to move into what Arnold Mindell (2001) calls level one, Dreamland, which is the land of roles, theories, and concepts. I began at level zero, which is the level of consensus reality and includes feelings and everyday observations. When I perform my inner work, or perhaps it is more realistic to say "when it occurs," I move from level one to level two, which is the level of conscious awareness. It is the level at which I see the interrelated systemic wholeness of the situation. The part of me that observes is awake. I am suddenly in a state of lucidity, an altered state. The world becomes different. I see the world through different eyes.

A participant in a presentation that I gave on the inner experience of the educator provided a good example of inner work. As part of his teacher certification, his supervisor came to watch him teach a grade-7 class. The next day the students were all giggling when he came in. He asked what was so funny. After a little hesitation, the students told him that that class had been the best class he had ever taught, saying that he was funny and made the lesson fun and how different it was from the usual classes. This teacher went away and reflected on this statement. He recalled his family experience which told him how important it was to be strict, calm, and controlled with children. This made sense to him in terms of his large family where the atmosphere was authoritarian, controlled, and contained and his parents' needs for order and decorum. He recognized that on the day his supervisor was present, his anxiety had moved him to be more excitable and emotive than he would usually be. He recognized how his family background had influenced him to become dull as a teacher, teaching as if he was heading his family of origin. Out of this experience he resolved to change his approach to teaching and to students, to be true to his feelings, to trust more in his students' desire to learn, and to optimize his and their potential to have a good experience in class. Crucial to his insight was the realization about the influence his family background had played in his approach to teaching and how his way of being in the classroom previously was inconsistent with his nature, which was fun loving and good humored. His inner work and its translation into practice combined to create a life changing experience.

Master Teachers and Inner Work

In this essay I set out to investigate what makes for an effective teacher, that is, a teacher who students find compelling. I have given my analysis in terms of inner work. The kind of effective teacher or master teachers about which I have written are those who have little or no gap between how they present themselves to be and who they are. The closing of the gap is the fruit of the inner work. In the remainder of the essay, my analysis of the master teacher is placed into a somewhat historical and cross-cultural—or, to be more precise, Eastern—perspective in order to further enrich and inform my view and perspective.

Durkheim (1975), the German philosopher and psychologist, spent his life interpreting Eastern thought for Westerners. He wrote about the need for the master teacher to assist the student in becoming aware of the master within themselves. In psychological terms, this would be a reference to the student's projection on to the master of his or her own capacities to be a master or masterful. In referring to the inner master, Durkheim says:

> There are always two levels on which master and student cooperate in bringing Being into existence in human shape: one is the external, contingent world, where master and student meet as real human beings—and the other is within the seeker himself. The master here is not an outside figure but an authority directing the student from within. Deep inside ourselves, we are all masters and students in this sense, and this is due to the anguish and strength of true nature, forcing its way within us toward self-realization in worldly form. But we must bring this fact to consciousness. Seek-

ing and finding the external master depends, like everything that master does, on the inner master. (pp. 34–35)

A major part of the task of the educator is to facilitate this contact with the inner master in each student and to nurture the growth process of mastery. Through this process, learners can be empowered to understand that they have undiscovered inner resources and capacities for learning and knowing. This undertaking is supported by the educator's inner work, modeling, facilitation of learning, and modeling and facilitation of learning about learning—learning that is about both self and curriculum content, encouragement, and education.

One of the most difficult things for many teachers to do is to sit patiently and even silently in wait for students to present themselves—to "show up." Too frequently, teachers talk too much and too loudly, making pronouncements of what students should know and need to know. In this vein, teachers often talk over students, and if students do not resist, which is the most common response, the teachers end up, more often than not, not talking to anyone, as the students have departed in terms of their capacity to attend to either their inner life or the outer world; to use common vernacular, they are "zoned out." Their self-awareness is gone. Their metacommunicator is shut down. They aren't going to discover their inner master in this condition. Master teachers are able to be quiet, but their quietness is not destructive to students' desire to participate and listen. In fact, it is reassuring and encouraging to students. Master teachers' whose silence represents inner stillness and awareness manifest "presence": a warm and spacious glow that extends to others and encourages their full presence. In the presence of such stillness, students come to a heightened awareness of their inner life and their metacommunicator, or witness consciousness. Full presence by the educator is in and of itself a confrontation about responsibility for students. Such presence does not involve any particular doing but the educator's way of being that includes the capability of presence. Such presence involves certain characteristics that I shall outline next.

Presence involves listening not only with ears and mind but also listening with heart, which means hearing the emotions and the essence of the persons who speak, *hearing* what is not said, and hearing those who do not speak overtly, and listening for what is in the quietness. For example, if there is emotion in the room and it is not given a voice, the task of the educational leader is to notice and acknowledge this voice that is silent and to create opportunity for the silence itself to have a voice. This allows for understanding of the implications, reason, and meaning of the particular silence and acknowledges and reinforces the value of inviting in the silenced parts of experience. This level of acknowledgment has its own value and is also a model of sensitivity to what might otherwise be marginalized for learners. An educational leader who exemplifies this type of heart awareness facilitates the leadership potential of students by example.

Mitchell's (Lao-tzu, 1988) translation of a chapter from the ancient text, the *Tao Te Ching*, captures something about a particular way of being present. It seems to be the way of near invisibility. In my own experience as a college instructor, if I wait and am attentive, students will often contribute what I might have said myself. Active presence on my part, along with facilitation, seems to be a crucial factor in the emergence of knowledge from students. My alertness ensures that I actively intervene at moments of transition, moments when I can add something that furthers learning, and moments of rupture or disjunction. The second meaning of presence is the capacity to be fully present in the moment. The consistent factors are that I am fully attentive and present to the best of my ability and that I am consistently working on developing my ability to attend and be present. The Tao Te Ching tells us:

> When the Master governs, the people
> are hardly aware that he exists...
> When his work is done,
> the people say, "Amazing;
> we did it, all by ourselves!" (Ch. 17)

In the introduction to his translation, Mitchell says,

> Lao-tzu's central figure is a man or woman whose life is in perfect harmony with the way things are. This is not an idea; it is a reality; I have seen it. The Master has mastered Nature; not in the sense of conquering it, but of becoming it. In surrendering to the Dao, in giving up all concepts, judgments, and desires, her mind has grown naturally compassionate. She finds deep in her own experience the central truths of the art of living, which are paradoxical only on the surface; that the more truly solitary we are, the more compassionate we can be; the more we let go of what we love, the more present our love becomes; the clearer our insight into what is beyond good and evil, the more we can embody the good. Until finally she is able to say, in all humility, 'I am the Tao, the Truth, the Life.' (pp. viii–ix)

This idea for guidance suggests that the educational leader will be deeply immersed in a process of inner work and trust; trust that what is natural will emerge if he or she does the work to remove the obstructions that block what is alive and natural, so that the Dao can make itself known, and so the educator can be more fully present. Further, this esoteric little chapter suggests that there is a relationship between the master and the people that are intrinsically related and relational and that involves a subtlety that both agree to in some way.

The master teacher has not forgotten concepts, judgments, and desires. In fact, he or she is very aware of them. However, the master teacher lives in a state of consciousness that is nonordinary. He or she sees these very commonplace experiences as components of a larger field. Because the master teacher's presence is authentic—there is no gap between the teacher's presentation of self and his or her inner feeling—he or she is able to see what is before him or her without any interruption of vision, feeling, or thought that would create a distortion between the outer reality and the inner perception. He or she sees and knows the background within which these experiences exist and is not pushed, pulled, and unduly influenced by them. He or she, as an outcome of inner work, is simultaneously of, with, and in the world while maintaining a vantage point that knows and sees all the components in a feeling way and also their interblending. This is achievable through an ongoing process of inner work practice and is a necessary undertaking for the emergence of the true teacher. I would add that it is in and through this unending pursuit that the true teacher emerges. This emergence and the capacity for presence are profoundly connected. There is no final moment of achievement. It is a life-long process.

The master teacher has a highly evolved capacity to recognize and live in the space and place of inter-being (Hahn, 2001), a nonordinary state of being, between self and all things. Lao-tzu suggests that the master governs and that he or she does it while exercising the subtle art of transparency, which at times seems to approach invisibility. When the master teacher is transparent, he or she is actively and clearly involved but in a way that is in the service of bringing forth the emerging knowledge that seems to have a life of its own within the group. As the master's visibility decreases, the learner community moves into the foreground. The master teacher is quiet and may even be forgotten, at least in the moment, by the students as they discover their knowledge and resources. There is no sense of causality. The master may be in the role of facilitator, and at times, the learner community has this role. According to Arnold Mindell (2002),

> One of the distinguishing characteristics of process-oriented organizational work, and its application to group meetings…is the special combination of inner and outer 'awareness work.' Process-oriented facilitation works with our inner lives and dreams, as well as with group life, and its dreams and stories. (p. ix)

The implication is that the students have the requisite knowledge and skills within and that the master teacher role facilitates emergence of what is available and wanting to emerge. The students have an increasing awareness that they are the agents of creation. The *timespirit* of the facilitator is significant and contains the possibility of being with and moving amongst the members of the community in a variety of ways. Specifically, the timespirit is seen as something separate from the person who may be enacting it at a given moment. The role of a teacher is a timespirit that he or she takes on and enacts and then drops when done with it. The master is in a continuous process of development and learning and may have a very fluid ability to pick up the timespirit of facilitator, let it go for another, and pick it up again. The creative emptiness of the master that results from inner work allows him or her to pick up a timespirit and then let it go while remaining completely open to the needs, requirements, and responses that present themselves at any given moment. Mastery and being a master teacher is really a commitment to a process. This process arises out of an increased experience of emptiness, which is an outcome of inner work.

EMPTINESS AND INNER EXPERIENCE

The idea of emptiness comes from Eastern religious traditions and practices. Nakagawa (2000) refers to "'wu' (nothingness or non-being) as the deepest ground, out of which all other dimensions emerge" (p.141). In the context of education, the educational leader's capacity for wu constitutes the ground for the emergence of the knowledge, both human and curricular, that exists within the learning community. This emptiness is neither a sign of something necessary lacking nor is it a static state. The emptiness within the educator is the opening of space, a generative opening that invites a creative flow and outpouring from the community of learners. An observer might see a teacher who is quieter than most teachers, who does not rush in to fill silences, who judiciously allows students to struggle to come to understanding, who offers questions and statements that are intended to bring forth what is in the student(s), and who does, at times, come forth with ideas and direction. An astute observer would notice that even when the master is more prominent, his or her presence is very often framed in a way that also evokes and provokes more opportunity for students to discover knowledge that they may not have been aware they had. He or she is also interested in having individual students spontaneously provide the information that other students do not have, which is simultaneously in the service of students discovering their power. All this can arise out of the master teacher's development of *wu-wei* that contributes to the development of mastery and develops through the process of attending to his or her inner experience.

No-Thing
I was no-thing
I will be no-thing
I am no-thing.
Who writes?
—a. cohen

HUMAN DEVELOPMENT, GROWTH, AND PRESENCE

The issue of personality bears mentioning at this point. Kirk Schneider (2004) says that much of personality is developed and preserved as a mask that serves as a shield to protect what he calls the *fluid center of life*, "any sphere of human consciousness which has as its concern the widest possible relationships to existence" (p. 10). What is masked is the person's authentic way of being. Their vulnerability and soft core of being, that was wounded a long time ago, is being shielded and protected. This soft core or fluid center of life is finely tuned to notice, unconsciously, that which confirms the need for a protective personality structure. Classrooms and counselors' offices are filled with people who have developed personalities that serve as protection rather than as a vehicle for authentic expression. Not surprisingly many of these people are the educators and counselors. The task of the educator and the counselor is to facilitate an unmasking process that encourages access to the soft core of being in himself or herself and in students and that optimizes the possibility of emergence of the person's most authentic way of being. This access is gained through moving ever deeper into the inner life.

I am not suggesting that it is necessary for an educator to be an enlightened master. The term *master* is better understood as a process of mastery development and suggests to me a person who intends to be present in each moment, to be more of who he or she is, and who is moving toward a perpetually receding horizon. Life continues until it doesn't. The suggestion is that within each person, there are potentials that are predisposed to emerge under the right conditions. The crucial action is one of stepping aside, becoming empty of any false sense of identity, to allow for the emergences of potential and knowledge that the learner has and has not yet realized. Such knowledge may exist only in seed form. Inner work is a process of personal reflection with the intention of growth of consciousness and associated self-expression and is crucial to what an optimal and continually developing educational environment requires. Some signs of consciousness growth include an enlarged capacity to see what is both visible and invisible, realization of a broader perspective than was previously apparent, an increased sense of space and ease within oneself, a felt sense of connection, and a sense of consciousness that is present in and, at the same time, transcends the moment. This listing of signs is incomplete and should not be understood as goals but only as markers along the way. The educator can be who the situation requires and still be in integrity with deeply held values.

Mastery indicates an ability to manifest a sense of presence. Presence is a concept with many meanings. Presence arises authentically out of *wu-wei*. In the same way that an empty bowl represents a potential to be filled, the true experience of emptiness is an experience of readiness and openness to whatever life offers. In this context, I mean a presence that integrates body, mind, and spirit.

The "job" of the master educator is to address and encourage the human spirit and to evoke or provoke the unconscious to bring the spiritual to consciousness and, consequently, to bring the idea of the spiritual and the associated choice to exist into consciousness. I believe that the atmosphere that is created by such an undertaking by the educator when it is done with passion, compassion, care, and skill creates an atmosphere where curriculum learning becomes practically inevitable.

DEEPER INTO THE INNER LIFE

What follows is a fictionalized compilation of experiences from my classes. One of my students tended, from my perspective, to be very dominating in classroom discussions. During a particular class, I was demonstrating facilitation of a group process with a subset of the class while the rest of the class observed with particular assigned tasks that would be used as discussion points after the demonstration. The exercise was designed to last 15 minutes. A student who was a member of the demonstration group began almost immediately to ask one of the other participants a series of interview-like questions.It seemed likely that this interviewing process could take up the whole time allotted for the demonstration, would exclude other students from active participation, was at odds with the guidelines that had been given, and would certainly impair the pedagogical intent. I was aware that he was very sensitive and tended to perceive anything that was not floridly positive as a personal criticism. I had to decide whether to let the process unfold as it was or to intervene. I chose the latter. The student stopped talking and was quiet for the remainder of the exercise and the rest of that class. Two days before the next class I received a phone message from this student saying that he had felt humiliated by my comments to him and that he could not return to class unless there was some resolution.

I had come away from this previous class filled with feelings of heaviness and anxiety. I felt that the demonstration and my intervention with this student had gone poorly. I was concerned about the effect on the rest of the class. Up to this point, the classes had been very lively, filled with personal sharing, connection, and dialogue about the course material, all of which had taken place in a supportive and encouraging atmosphere. Before returning the call, I sat in meditation (Cohen, 2002) and reflected upon what had occurred and, particularly, my experiences with this student. Here, I describe for you my experience in the present tense to give you, as much as possible, a sense of immediacy about my inner work.

> I need to get inside the experience of this person. I notice that I have reluctance. I find within me a strong feeling of dislike. I feel a tendency within me to move away. I listen to this tendency. I back up inwardly and am looking at

him from a distance. I see a large person who takes up a lot of psychological space and simultaneously conveys a message that seems to say, 'Excuse me, I don't want to cause a problem.' As I imagine him speaking, my body tenses and I feel fear arising in me. My body is becoming cold and my heart feels like it has a clamp on it that is being tightened. Suddenly, I have concerns about the class being taken over. I imagine extreme unhappiness emerging from the other students. Awareness of my fears leads quickly to my next concern that the class will be unsuccessful and that my view of myself as a good teacher will be altered. I also have an awareness of a fear-fantasy that the program director will be notified. I feel my common sense mind being overwhelmed by my fears for my professional and personal survival. I want to obliterate this student and appear blameless in the process.

This fantasy resided in my consciousness, constraining my capacity to respond and was the repetition of a habitual, somewhat unconscious, personal pattern. This experience of dread was preprogrammed from my personal history to occur under the right circumstances, and this event with this student constituted those right circumstances. The available time to work with all this was brief, but I knew that I had to do something in order to be able to communicate with this student and the class in a different and better way.

As I sit in the inner relationship with this student, I feel another ripple of fear. A childhood memory emerges. I am small. I am going to school. I have to cross the street with the assistance of the schoolboy patrol. The boy who is on duty is big, and I know that he has threatened and struck some children with his sign. I feel fear in my body. I feel its rush through me. I do not like the feeling and feel the beginnings of fear about having the fear. I recognize that I have been responding to this student with vestiges of this old feeling and, particularly, out of my unconscious effort to avoid feeling this fear. As a small child I need reassurance. My early mentor, Dr. Peter Lavelle, appears. I hear his voice. He says, 'You are sitting on your own power. You are afraid of what you might do and the effects of your power.' Somehow, I know that this ties in with my fears of being alone. My child mind knows that if I am strong and forceful, others will move away. Another childhood memory surfaces. I am about 8 and I am playing a game with other children. I make a quick move that changes the whole direction of the game in my favor. I notice that the children draw back. Nothing is said, but viscerally I know that I am being rejected because of my power in this situation.

My power in this situation and in classrooms is attributed power and is not power that I intrinsically have or that actually gives me authority over anyone. It is attributed to the position of instructor by me, students, institutions, personal history, and society. In psychoanalytic terms, it is a complex combination of transference, countertransference, and projective identification. Briefly, transference refers to projection from personal history by the patient on to the analyst. Here, I am borrowing the term and applying it to the projections of learners onto the educator. Countertransference, similarly, is the projection onto learners individually and collectively by the educator. Projective identification is the unconscious assignment of a role that is then taken up unconsciously by the educator. An example would be as follows: A student who has issues about being dominated by authority figures sees the educator as an authority figure. The student behaves in ways that draw out of the educator domineering behavior even though this is not a part of the educator's usual way of being. Both are caught in an unconscious relationship that arises out of the student's issue and the educator's unconsciousness.

> As a child, I know viscerally that how and who I am has consequences that are frightening. Surprisingly, calmness starts to sweep over me. I realize that I am doing to myself what I have experienced as a child and reactively blaming this student who is troubling for me. I know what I have to do; nothing. *Wu-wei* is emerging. My inner tension and fear has been replaced with a feeling of warmth and curiosity and is, I believe, what will make the difference for me and this student.

I phoned the student and was able to be quiet and listen receptively to his concerns and fears. He relaxed as the conversation proceeded. He thanked me for listening and allowing him to express himself without interruption and "for not making me wrong."

This is a detailed articulation of my work with my inner life as a human being who assumes the timespirit of educator. To catch and identify these moments of importance requires awareness and cat-like quickness. Creating time and space for this type of reflection has been personally meaningful and has transformed professional practice possibilities. Experiences can be taken into this stronghold of inner reflection, and the inner work outcomes can be brought back into the classroom in an ongoing interactive practice. In this way, the self-care needs, the growth of the educator and learners, the human needs, and desires to absorb the curriculum can be optimally attended to.

IN THE END/THE BEGINNING

I think the case for inner work is actually easily made. Philosophically determinism states that an individual's actions are predetermined by existing conditions. I suggest that most human behavior is determined by the imposition of personal history that has formed a person's personality and ways of being into hardened forms and that the wellspring from which these forms have sprung and the awareness that they even came from this source has long been buried in a person's unconscious. Most of human behavior is to a great extent determined or, to use current technological language, programmed. The way out of this deterministic trap and toward free will requires that a person free themselves from the influence of these unconscious forces. The way to foster this freeing is through contemplation on and work with the inner world—work that involves shining the light of consciousness into the shadow of that which is out of awareness and bringing these processes into awareness. This inner work liberates energy, potential, and capacities and talents that have been buried under the rubble of pressure to conform in the service of survival. I need to add that all freedom is limited in terms of actions as the world has a limiting effect. The only limits on inner freedom in terms of consciousness are the limits that are buried in the unconscious of the person.

Involvement in the process of exploring and understanding my inner life and finding ways to translate this into practice that includes increasing my capacity to be fully present is an ongoing and essential part of my life as an educator[10] and a counselor.[11] The inner life of the educator and the ability to work with this aspect of consciousness is a vital feature of education. I believe this dimension is not attended to sufficiently by educators or policy makers in the educational system and that this is costly to learners, educators, and society. This statement derives from my knowledge that methods for attending to the inner life are not part of the curriculum for educating educators and hearing from educators who are struggling with the effects of not having these skills. The educator's attention or lack of attention along with his or her ability to work with these inner experiences will either enhance or detract from the educational community, individual learners, and learning.

Inner experience is the internal representation and experience of phenomena. Attention to, identification of, and expression of inner experience increases the possibility that an educator will connect with individual students and the community of students in ways that optimize the development of community and learning. Such attention can identify moments of rupture or rapture, the associated phenomena, and the inner work that allows the authentic self out of its prison and into its truest path. A crucial step in the process is noticing internal experiences. An educator who has access, curiosity, a commitment to inner experience, and insight into the deepest meanings of their experience, offers inspiration to learners that is essential to igniting their desire to learn. Is that not crucial to education and development of learners who are the future?

LATER

I am out for a run. I am thinking about this essay. A fantasy about my death emerges. The following poetic response to the whole process emerges:

Academic/Death Comes Running

The news arrives,
I will be dying.

I run
The sweat pours off me.

I must finish my work.
The academy becomes very human,
Special arrangements are made.

I feel my body move.

Even the President of the University
All there...
Death creates human flesh out of the institutional
skeleton.
I die before I die.

Feeling deep emotion.

Join me here
In the heart of the matter...

Learning to hear the sound of my beating Heart,
Engaging senses,
Smelling the Blood of my Heart,
Tasting the Blood,
Becoming Blood...

In the midst of the silence of the Way............

REFERENCES

Cohen, A. (2002, April). The secret of effective psychotherapy: Metaskills. *The Private Practitioner Bulletin of the Canadian Counselling Association, 1*(3), 3.

Cohen, A. (2002). *Whole person meditation: Introductory manual.* Vancouver, BC, Canada: Life Force.

Durkheim, K. G. (1975). *The call for the master: The meaning of spiritual guidance on the way to the self.* Toronto, ON, Canada: Fitzhenry & Whitehead.

Fuller, R.W. (2003). *Somebodies and nobodies: Overcoming the abuse of rank.* Gabriola Island, BC, Canada: New Society Publishers.

Hahn, T. N. (2001). *Thich Nhat Hahn: Essential writings.* Maryknoll, NY: Orbis Books.

Ladinsky, D. (1999). *The gift: Poems by Hafiz, the great Sufi master.* Toronto, ON, Canada: Penguin.

Lao-tzu. (1988). *Tao te ching* (S. Mitchell, Trans.). New York: Harper & Row.

Miller, J. (1988). *Spiritual pilgrims.* Unpublished manuscript, Toronto, ON, Canada.

Miller, J. P. (1996). *The holistic curriculum.* Toronto, ON: OISE.

Mindell, Arnold. (1990/1991). *Inner dreambody work: Working on yourself alone.* Portland, OR: Lao Tse Press.

Mindell, Arnold. (1994/2001). *Metaskills: The spiritual art of therapy.* Portland, OR: Lao Tse Press.

Mindell, Arnold. (1995). *Sitting in the fire: Large group transformation using conflict and diversity.* Portland, OR: Lao Tse Press.

Mindell, Arnold. (2001). *The dreammaker's apprentice: Using heightened states of consciousness to interpret dreams.* Charlottesville, VA: Hampton Roads.

Mindell, Arnold. (2002). *The deep democracy of open forums: Practical steps to conflict prevention and resolution for the family, workplace, and world.* Charlottesville, VA: Hampton Roads.

Murphy, M. (1993). *The future of the body: Explorations into the further evolution of human nature.* New York: Putnam.

Nakagawa, Y. (2000). *Education for awakening: An eastern approach to holistic education.* Brampton, ON, Canada: Foundation for Educational Renewal.

Palmer, P. (1990). *The active life: A spirituality of work, creativity, and caring.* New York: Harper.

Palmer, P. (1998). *The courage to teach: Exploring the inner landscape of a teacher's life.* San Francisco: John Wiley & Sons.

Schneider, K. J. (2004). *Rediscovery of awe: Splendor, mystery, and the fluid center of life.* St. Paul, MN: Paragon House.

Schumacher, E. F. (1999). *Small is beautiful: Economics as if people mattered.* Point Roberts, WA: Hartley & Marks. (Original work published 1973)

Schumacher, E. F. (1997). *This I believe and other essays.* Devon, U.K.: Green Books.

Talmor, R., Seiter, S., & Feigin, N. (2005). Factors relating to regular education. *European Journal of Special Needs Education, 20*(2), 215–229.

CHAPTER 4

CLASSROOM AS COMMUNITY: DEEP DEMOCRACY PRACTICE

One
The sound of one hand clapping
Is not so awesome as it used to be.
I now listen for the sound of
Ten thousand hands clapping as One.
—Lao-Tzu's Protégé[12]
——a. cohen

I know that the Bachelor of Education students I work with want me to tell them how to manage the chaos of the classroom, how to keep order, but I want my student-teachers to acknowledge the chaos of the classroom because in acknowledging the chaos of the classroom they will be able to live in productive and transformative relationship with their students and colleagues. Otherwise they will know only frustration and disappointment and defeat because they will never match their dreams of order with the dis/order that characterizes the lived and living experience(s) of schools. Instead of fearing the wildness of chaos and grasping any semblance of cosmos, I encourage my student-teachers to explore the lines of connection between cosmos and chaos as chiasmata where the lines create a crosswise intersection and fusion, perhaps finding even the enfolding of cosmos in chaos and chaos in cosmos.

—Leggo (1998, pp. 173–174)

When you have means of reflecting on yourself, then you do not lose sight of the conditions and feelings of others. If you have no means of reflecting on yourself, then confusion comes into play when you act.

—Cleary (1991, p. 130)

In this essay I will provide an overview of the appr oach that I developed and employed to teach counseling skills in a group. The method has multiple goals including learning process-oriented counseling skills, gaining integrated experiential and conceptual knowledge, personal growth, learning about group process and development, and the connection between individual and group growth. I will describe the approach to learning, not the counselling method itself, although the approach is reflective of the counselling method. As well, I will describe some basic assumptions about this approach, the training group as a community development experience, some process-oriented terminology, skills for those in facilitator and leadership positions, ideas about diversity, and individual differences, participants and the selection process, group structure and development, the relationship between the personal or emotional environment and the physical environment, the leader's attention to relationship details and self-care, learning methods and related ideas, ethical considerations, personal growth and personal therapy, and deep democracy which, in contrast to the traditional concept of democracy where power is based on numbers, facilitates inclusive dialogue based on the conviction that voices from the margins have an important message for the group as a whole. I will also describe deep democracy as a contrast to usual democracy where half a group plus one can dominate the entire group. Deep democracy attends to all the voices and seeks to facilitate a dialogue that is inclusive and incorporates the voices from the minority and the margins. Deep democracy values the message these voices have as important for the group as a whole.

Groups are like a microcosm of life—a community unfolding—and represent a great possibility of what can be (Cohen, 2003). Groups can demonstrate the best of human potential and, alternatively, all too often, the worst. A group in which training takes place can provide a lived model of optimal possibilities for participants. Every person carries in their unconscious an archetypal image of community. Every group simultaneously represents the possibility of a step toward this inner model and the possibility of a further integration of the inner community of disowned parts in the individual. War and peace are outcomes of what happens in groups and between them. Any constructive learning about relationships, groups, and ourselves is a potential step forward in the evolution of humanity and consciousness. Ideally a group within which counselors are trained will demonstrate and further these possibilities through the training provided in the content and structure provided within each meeting and throughout the entire training experience and in modeling the process itself.

Groups have the potential to expose and express those things that usually take place privately between people in a public space. In the process-directed educational environment that I have developed, communication is about personal and curriculum matters with group members as witnesses and participants. In this approach, both the feelings and the ideas that arise are dealt with as integrated parts of the group's work. The opportunity to learn from all the members of the group in an interrelated academic and personal way is a central characteristic of this approach.

The program is experientially and conceptually based. The program provides hands-on experience, personal growth opportunity, descriptive language, counseling skills, and a conceptual framework. Feedback is encouraged and is part of the ongoing process of evaluation and change and creates a lived experience that is reflective of the counseling model. Participants have invariably described these training experiences as meaningful and, in some cases, life changing. I have used the process-oriented approach to education in groups in academic and nonacademic environments, and in this essay I focus on a program to teach process-oriented counseling skills. My intent is to convey the essence of an experience that has been invariably positive.

The conceptual framework is drawn from counseling theory and practice. A process orientation in groups (Cohen, 1996a, 1996b; Arnold Mindell, 1992, 1995) that is consistent with viewing events within space and time as a systemic totality (Bateson & Bateson, 1988) is preferred over, but does not exclude, focusing on the individuals within the context. From a gestalt framework (Perls, Hefferline, & Goodman, 1951), there is attention to the background process, and work is done with this element to facilitate integration, growth, and learning. Invitation to examine the potential of the shadow (Jung, 1989) encourages looking into personal material that is avoided in most educational approaches. The existential approach (Frankl, 1985) is embedded in the program with continual encouragement to look for personal meaning and to follow what is most passionate for the learner. Learning is about and from these diverse perspectives. There is an ongoing interactive developmental process between the group and the individuals.

Development of the whole person is basic to the approach and includes the emotional, intellectual, physical, and spiritual dimensions. Support for the emergence of a person's true nature is an intrinsic part of the training. Palmer (1998) says about therapy, "Good methods can help a therapist find a way into the client's dilemma, but good therapy does not begin until the real-life therapist joins with the real life of the client" (p. 5). The ongoing discovery of this "real-life" therapist is a major aspect of the training.

In the training experience, a distinction is made between doing and being. Most of education is concerned with content and goal achievement, that is, doing. In this approach, the emphasis is on being but not to the exclusion of doing. The intent is to work toward a seamless integration of the two. The idea of being refers to the person who performs an action. Being includes the in-the-moment experience, their sense of identity, and their awareness.

There is a strong emphasis on contact and intimacy. Multidimensional communication construction in the moment (Cohen, 2004) is the "critical dimension of excellent communication that will lead to meaningful dialogue, contact, and increased intimacy is the ability to listen and express simultaneously" (p. 3). This includes possibilities of contacts that are intellectual, emotional, kinaesthetic, visual, auditory, and spiritual. The experience of intimacy and contact within multiple realms of interaction potentiate complex human encounters, and over an extended time frame, rare levels of intimacy can be cocreated.

Fehr (2003) quotes a participant in a therapy group about "the necessity of being constantly aware of what may seem to be even the most minor of interactions or events, as these may be clues to some underlying issues which should be examined" (p. 31). This statement suggests that in any group there are significant underlying dynamics and processes. A group trained for this level of sensitivity becomes an ongoing laboratory and experience of the topics addressed in the training. Personal material that arises is available for use as part of the learning process.

BASIC ASSUMPTIONS

I believe that students want to learn and have a capacity and desire for self direction. I assume that the educator is knowledgeable, passionate, and interested in the subject matter and in learners as students and as human beings. The educator's role is to facilitate student interest and their sense of belonging to the educational community. Metaphorically, the educator might think of himself or herself as an alchemist whose task is to tend to the raw material of the ground of the student's not knowing and create the conditions within which the transformation to gold is optimal on both a personal and academic level. The educator facilitates creative and meaningful personal and academic connections between students. This task includes attending to the flow of experience, in a sense being a Daoist; noticing when things are working well; keeping the space protected and flowing; and noticing when there is a lack of flow and, in those circumstances, attending to the knots of experience and facilitating their undoing. The educator has two primary tools: awareness and facilitation skills.

In this essay I use the terms *educator*, *facilitator*, and *leader* somewhat interchangeably. These three roles can be described as tendencies of emphasis with different emphases emerging as the situation dictates. *Educator* suggests the person who has responsibility for access to specific and expert knowledge. *Facilitator* is the role that supports learners in their humanness and the group's efforts to work together to discover knowledge. *Leader* is the role that points the learners and the learning in certain directions. Each role is important. The ability of the person to embody and move fluidly between roles will impact the learning of the group.

THE TRAINING GROUP AS A COMMUNITY DEVELOPMENT EXPERIENCE

My ideas about training in groups developed out of my experience working with adolescents in residential treatment where a modified version of Jones' (1968) ideas, which I describe in the upcoming text, about therapeutic community were employed. I saw that disturbed adolescents could make effective use of this approach and that staff members were even more adept with it. The benefits in terms of communication, collaboration, and community development were apparent. From there, I went on to extract the essence of these ideas for use in nontherapy contexts, particularly educational environments where I found that the approach was highly facilitative on human and pedagogical levels.

The training is framed as taking place within a developing community. This provides a significant part of the learning and is fostered by facilitating the relationships between participants. The relationships are seen as real. The feelings for each other and the relationships are valued. Projection and transference issues also arise and are used within the context of the group as learning opportunities and part of the community's experience.

The community development process includes encouragement of expression of a range of feelings and ideas. Learning to express, receive, and respond to feelings and ideas is valued. For example, there is encouragement and modeling of expressions of anger, for taking unpopular positions, and for standing in the heat. Conflict is valued as an opportunity for growth, and methods are demonstrated in the context of the group.

This is different to most educational groups where conflict is frequently avoided and seen as detrimental to the educational process. The leader recognizes and creates opportunities to learn about working with conflict and the potential to grow and create intimacy through such experience.

As Miller (1993) states, "community implies connection among beings" (p. 119). The group is a community in development. Jones (1968) captures the essence of what is desired when he says, "The democratic, egalitarian structure of a therapeutic community.... becomes a sort of living laboratory where crises, instead of being seen as troublesome and unnecessary, can be turned to good effect as learning situations" (pp. 10–11).

Jones goes on to describe the possibilities inherent in a therapeutic community and some attributes of leadership that he deems important:

> A therapeutic community, by attempting to make use of the optimal potential...and by creating learning situations where this potential may be developed, represents both a goal...and a philosophy. This situation calls for leadership with sensitivity to the needs of others...the capacity to develop potential becomes the most important aspect of leadership... The most important attribute of a leader in this context is his capacity to preserve the wholeness of an organization, while at the same time encouraging flexibility, self-examination, social learning, and change. (pp. 25–26)

Jones is a seminal thinker and pioneer in his work with this model of groups and organizational structure. If this model is workable in a psychiatric setting where it was developed, then, as has been my experience, surely those who are not subject to such extreme states can make even better use of this approach. These ideas embody the highest principles of respect for individual uniqueness, integrity, responsibility, and potential.

Yalom (1995) talks about the dual tasks of any group:

> First they must determine a method of achieving their primary task—the purpose for which they joined the group. Second, they must attend to their social relationships in the group so as

> to create a niche for themselves that will not only provide the comfort necessary to achieve their primary task but will also result in additional gratification from the sheer pleasure of group membership. (p. 295)

In a training group, as in therapy groups, the two tasks are overlapping, informative of each other, and facilitative of the group's development as a community. Relationships that developed between participants have continued beyond the training group as living testimony to the connection that develops between participants.

DEEP DEMOCRACY, ISSUES OF DIVERSITY, AND INDIVIDUAL DIFFERENCES

"Deep democracy" as described by Arnold Mindell (1992, 2002) is employed in the training program. Arnold Mindell (1992) writes:

> Deep democracy touches upon all levels of our lives. In personal life, it means openness to all of our inner voices, feelings, and movements, not just the ones we know and support, but also the ones we fear and do not know well... In group life it means the willingness to listen to and experiment with whatever part comes up. In global work, deep democracy values politics, ethnicity, and the spirit of nature. (pp. 154–155)

The practices of deep democracy address issues of diversity, which means acknowledging intellectually and experientially details of individual and group experience. The idea that each person has something to offer and has an obligation to do so is endemic to the developing culture. A similar view is taken about the parts of the self that are disavowed or hidden from view. Nuances of experience are seen as aspects of the whole, and the practice of deep democracy suggests the commitment to and practice of accessing those parts and including them in the process.

An example involves a man who was deathly afraid of speaking in the training group. For many weeks he said as little as possible and concealed his fear. He eventually shared with me that he had this fear. We discussed the possibilities for addressing this. I suggested that he could say something about it, tell someone else, and have that person share his fear; I could say something; or he could continue as he had been doing with an emphasis on self-reflection to learn more about the process. He decided that he would share this fear in the next group during the opening group process. The group was very interested and supportive. Others with similar fears shared their experience. Most importantly, there was a shift. His dilemma became the group's dilemma. His silence was seen as a loss for the group. Whatever he might have to share was not available. Questions arose. What was it about our group that fed the fear? What could we do about it? How could we track the process? This man became a representative of the silent and fearful part of everyone. His response was quite emotional. This process unfolded over a couple of months, became part of the group's oral history, and culminated with him coming to the group one evening dressed up in a costume and performing a piece of theatre for the group that involved the group as audience and participants. Essentially the identified problem—fear of speaking out—became a seed experience for individual growth, community development, and an example of a deeply democratic process.

SOME PROCESS-ORIENTED TERMINOLOGY: EDGES, METASKILLS, RESISTANCE, AND ROLES

Awareness of personal edges is a significant aspect of the program. Edge is defined by Arnold Mindell (1998) as "the experience of not being able to do something, being limited or hindered from accomplishing, thinking, or communicating" (p. 175). A person's known identity does not encompass the experience that exists beyond a personal edge. *Metaskills* are the ongoing continuously unfolding and emerging in-the-moment feelings and attitudes that are reflective of the most deeply held beliefs of the counsellor. If accessed in a naturalistic way the enactment of these metaskills will bring the process to life in ways the use of techniques that are applied in a mechanical way cannot (Cohen, 2002; Amy Mindell, 1995).

Resistance is seen as significant information that is trying to emerge that is important for individuals and the group. This differs from the predominant view in the counseling field that views resistance as an impediment to be removed. Resistance can be broken down into two parts. One part is trying to do, be, or see something, and the other oppositional part is against this. Both have value. The relationship between them is antagonistic and the work involves uncovering the intent of each and opening up a communicative dialogue between them with the idea that seeds of growth reside within the troubling experience. Resistance is the inner other and can no more be eradicated than the other in an interpersonal conflict.

Roles are viewed as temporary, complex experiences that say something about a person in the moment and do not define a person's identity. Roles in groups may be represented or not. Ghost roles—any nonpresent other—can exist in the group's atmosphere and have a powerful influence. Identification of and work with roles are basic to the group's process and learning.

LEADERSHIP AND FACILITATOR SKILLS

It is important for the leader to have and demonstrate four skills that are basic for the group and individual therapist:

1. The capacity to attend to another's experience.
2. The ability to accept another person's experience and to convey that acceptance.
3. The ability to demonstrate a range of metaskills.
4. The ability to facilitate the creation of a containment field, for the group's process, emotions, and connections.

As well, the group leader makes use of four categories of multilevel awareness:

1. Split awareness: paying attention to what is going on in the foreground while maintaining an awareness of background processes.

An example would be performing a demonstration while checking on the group.

2. Dual awareness: tracking the external process while keeping in tune with internal processes both in response to what is occurring and as potential input for the group. For example, I might notice that a participant speaks animatedly, and simultaneously, I experience a warm feeling.

3. Role awareness: maintaining awareness of roles as they emerge, the effect of the roles, and role shifts as they occur and how. For example if I become very absorbed in an interaction, I could say, "I am now stepping out of the role of facilitator as I would like to participate in this interaction. Could someone agree to take the role of facilitator?"

4. Self-reflective awareness: the capacity to notice, reflect, perform inner work, evaluate, and articulate experience. I could say to a quiet participant, "I am aware that when you get quiet, I feel a sense of anticipation. When I was a child and my brother got quiet, his quietness was usually followed by a funny comment."

A group leader facilitates a group through the stages of group development, including an ability to work with the *chaos* of beginning, the intimacy and working through the process of the middle stage, and the work with the ending of the group and using these experiences as learning opportunities about these stages. The leader needs to have an ability to track the process of both the group and individuals and to tie this in with large group themes and processes as these develop and emerge. Conversely, the leader can help the group see the interactive relationship between group processes and the processes of individuals. The leader is alert for a new metaposition—the position that facilitates the group taking increasing responsibility for itself. As the group participants take over more of the maintenance of the group, the leader, at times, shifts to the role of group consultant.

It is crucial that the leader has a great interest in being in groups, leading groups, relationship and intimacy, the whole process of counselling, and working on himself. This makes a substantial contribution to the atmosphere of the group and also models metaskills that are significant in a group setting and work with individuals. After leading one program I received feedback that participants were surprised that I hadn't spoken more. I think that this is rare feedback for an educator and speaks to the resources within the group and the value of the leader as the facilitator.

PARTICIPANTS AND THE SELECTION PROCESS

The participants in this program come from diverse backgrounds and generally each student has been through a life crisis that has led to a personally meaningful process of personal reflection. They know the territory from the inside. Participants meet certain criteria including the ability to be relational in a group, a capacity to meta-communicate (talk about) their experience, a capacity to attend to another person, a substantial interest in the self and others, a desire to work with people, a willingness and ability to be in the presence of strong emotions, sufficient capacity for and interest in intimate relationships over time, and a potential for being with people in creative, unique, and unusual ways. As well, the participants need to have adequate abilities and an interest in participating in a group that interweaves a training function and a personal growth dimension. Participants come with a variety of agendas. They want to learn the skills for use in organizational, professional, and personal environments.

An interactive interview is set up as a process of mutual discovery. Information about the program, the underlying philosophy, my role as leader or facilitator, and description of the experiential nature of the program is shared. Opportunity is provided for the applicant to talk about their personal and professional background and their reasons for pursuing this type of training. During the interview, at some points, I will focus on the present, be self-disclosing, and articulate my passion for the work. The interview experience is reflective of the training process. Feedback is given to applicants, and the applicant is left with information to consider about the implications of joining the group.

GROUP STRUCTURE AND DEVELOPMENT

To liberate a free-flowing creative process, structure is used as a scaffold and not as a recipe for the group's activities. An example of the use of structure is that timing, sequence, and content of various elements are consistent for each meeting. The purpose of the structural component is to support the learning process. This is unlike some educational approaches where it is used to control or oppress expression. Content of particular program elements within allotted, predictable, and consistent time frames is supported. On rare occasions when circumstances suggest a change to timing as structured, this becomes part of the group's process and supports ownership of changes. The clarity and consistency of the structure, along with process-oriented facilitation, supports the maintenance of balance between process and content issues—which is often a concern in groups—and frees the group to attend to the content of learning.

The group meets over a 9-month period, one evening per week for 4 hours, along with four weekends spaced evenly throughout the program. During the first term of the program, all practice is in the form of in-class experiential exercises. In the second term, this continues, and additionally students are paired with each other for practice outside of class time.

Along with the group sessions, each student has three individual supervision opportunities with the facilitator to discuss their work. The content for these sessions is mutually defined.

The first hour of each meeting is devoted to group process for which guidelines (Cohen, 1996a) are provided. Participants can check in with their in-the-moment experience, share experiences, give and receive feedback, learn experientially about conflict in groups, perform individual or relationship work in the group, experience the development of this group as community, learn experientially about group intimacy, and learn about their effect on the group and the converse. Twenty minutes is then devoted to understanding and conceptualizing the process. Included in the possibilities for discussion are the facilitation, roles, group dynamics, the developmental stage of the group, the meaning of experiences, and transitions.

Next there is a presentation about the learning focus for the session and relevant related material from the manual (Cohen, 1996b) is discussed. An experiential exercise is introduced, including a 15-minute demonstration with a volunteer from the group. This is followed with an opportunity for feedback, discussion, and questions. Partners are then chosen to try the method. One hour is allotted for this, and participants try the roles of counselor, client, and, in some exercises, observer. The time is divided equally with a 5-minute debrief at each transition point. Then the group comes back together for discussion and feedback. Finally 15 minutes are devoted to putting closure on the entire session on a personal and didactic level.

The initial sessions are used to outline and establish the structure and culture of the group, work with beginning issues, and start learning the material. The structure as just described is established at the outset, maintained throughout the program, and looks after basic issues related to time, safety, and predictability, while maximizing creative possibilities.

In the middle stage the group's understanding and skill development deepens, intimacy grows, risk taking increases, and identification and development of the group's culture is central. Group members focus on their own issues, the current learning tasks, working in a co-creative mode, the potential of conflict as an opening to increased intimacy, developing a sense of safety and history, identifying and being in an ongoing process of identifying group patterns, having what is for most a different experience of intimacy, discovering the group's unique character and culture, and learning about their individual and collective ways of being in group.

In the final stage the focus is on issues related to ending. Group members can deal with issues related to this ending, other endings in their lives, reviewing and evaluating this experience, cultural background related to endings, giving and receiving feedback, unfinished business, and looking to the future. Kubler-Ross' (1969) model related to death and dying, including denial, anger, bargaining, sadness, and acceptance, is used as a frame for the ending. For many in the group, it is an opportunity to process an ending in a way that is new.

The participants generally have a parallel experience between their personal growth and their work to learn counselling skills. Initially they struggle to comprehend the basics. In the middle stage they have moved towards an attitude of experimentation and curiosity and are less concerned with getting things 'right'. In the ending stage they are experiencing the fruits of their labours, and work on fine tuning, acknowledging, or taking care of unfinished business of both a personal and skills nature.

THE RELATIONSHIP BETWEEN THE PERSONAL AND THE PHYSICAL ENVIRONMENT

The personal and emotional environment is highly valued and nurtured, and this is conveyed by sensitive attention to the details of associated issues. Extensive attention is given to possible events that could affect the environment. Doors are closed or locked, phone ringers are off, and "do not disturb" signs are in place. Outsiders are only brought in by invitation and with permission from the group, absences and returns are acknowledged, and participants are asked to communicate about absences. This ongoing attention to detail supports a feeling of safety and predictability in the group. This environmental sensitivity consecrates the space as sacred. Participants feel connected to each other, that their learning is valued, and that the events of their lives and their feelings matter.

THE LEADER'S ATTENTION TO RELATIONSHIP DETAILS AND SELF-CARE

A leader is a role model. As leader, by my way of being, I want to convey my care and concern for the community and the individual learners. I want to develop a realistic bond with each student that provides insight into what kinds of connections will nurture that individual's growth and learning. Where appropriate, contact is made outside the group with a participant to facilitate learning, to provide personal support, and to support the group's process. There is a constant interplay between the needs of the individual learners and the group as a whole. The fact of this contact is transparent even though the content may be confidential.

As leader, I endeavor to model the values that the program seeks to represent. I attend to what I call the 'three basics,'—adequate rest, good nutrition, and optimal physical activity—along with my emotional well-being. I also attempt to demonstrate appropriate limits in terms of my time and energies. Classes begin and end on time. Breaks occur on schedule. The benefit to participants of this self-care is to have a leader who is fit to offer the material that students have come to learn and whose way of being models self-care.

LEARNING METHODS AND RELATED IDEAS

Every aspect of the training group's structure, process, and content are designed to provide integrated learning opportunities. Diverse learning styles are addressed by the use of a contiguous variety of learning approaches, including written material, discussion, demonstrations, didactic presentations, feedback, and experiential exercises. Learning opportunities are available in groups, one to one, and on their own. Students are encouraged to identify their dominant and non-dominant learning styles, contexts that are easier and the converse for them, and to work with development and integration of these.

I have discovered intuitively that integration involves a here and now focus on experience, followed by a self-reflective opportunity to facilitate change and learning. This is consistent with Yalom's (1995) work even though his focus is on therapeutic learning. These two dimensions of learning become part of the group's culture and values.

ETHICAL CONSIDERATIONS

Pierce and Baldwin (1990) write,

> group leadership training in a counsellor education program must be fair, do no harm, respect the individual's right as a free agent

and yet at the same time, do them some good in being able to participate constructively and to use and control self-disclosure effectively. (p. 149)

I believe that these principles are also applicable to learning individual therapy in groups. The emphasis is on the protection of students. There are no balancing comments about the benefits of risk taking. I suggest student interests are best served where there is ample and appropriate support for risk taking. This is a component of process-oriented groups.

Ethical and legal considerations for this program include the contractual agreement and multilevel relationships, which combine learning with personal growth, confidentiality, and the use of personal material of participants as part of the learning process. There is a fine line to be walked in using individual participant's personal material as grist for the learning process. Within the program, the group has the opportunity to experience the complexity of working in this way, to learn about the sensitivity required, and to learn about all the potentials and implications of this way of working.

PERSONAL GROWTH AND PERSONAL THERAPY

Yalom (1995) points out the distinction between a therapy group and a group that is therapeutic. Participants in a group that is therapeutic are told that the leader cannot attend to them in the way that would be done in a therapy group. The use of methods associated with counseling is distinguished from counseling as a specific undertaking. In my experience, this is a common confusion. Using relational language, giving feedback, expressing feelings, and speculating about inner processes and interactional dynamics are methods that are used in counseling, but their use does not create a counseling process. In this training context, the approaches are used to facilitate the creation of a good educational environment and to demonstrate their use. The possibility of therapeutic benefits and personal growth is evident and common, but it is not the identified purpose of the group. The group's purpose is education, and the learning of these methods includes demonstration of their use.

Participants are encouraged to seek personal therapy outside the group to facilitate personal growth; to heal personal, emotional wounds; to learn about the therapy process by experience; and to support optimal use of the training group experience.

CONCLUDING THOUGHTS

The distinctions between this and other approaches are embedded in the attitude toward learners, which includes direct and consistent finely tuned attention to their humanity, with an emphasis on development of the educational community as an event in itself and as part of the learning process and the integration of curriculum and personal dimensions. I have described how the leader's role is to facilitate learning, encourage the potential of learners, and model the values, including responsiveness to learners and their communication and how the educational leader's role is one that can be described as continually changing and being redistributed as different leadership aspects are picked up by group members.

In the development of process-oriented learning communities, participants increasingly feel part of something substantial and part of something that they want to be a member of and also that it is something within which they feel agency and ownership. The groups are designed to create a feeling of emotional safety, enhance personal growth possibilities, skill learning opportunities, and to be comprehensive and holistic. There is a focus on the personal and the curricular, the individual and the group, and issues of diversity. The success of these groups derives from the process-oriented framework and the ability of the leader to implement the principles and methods of this approach. The distinguishing feature in these training groups is the lived curriculum that is the interactive responsiveness of the learners, including the educational leader to the material and, most importantly, to each other.

Finally, there is an implication of process-oriented learning communities for educational practice to be more broadly conceived. In contrast to more traditional educational practice, there is a shift in the power dynamics from leader focused to group focused, a living experience of acknowledging the other, actual engagement with issues of diversity, willingness to acknowledge and engage with the personal dimension, a focus on questions about meaning and purpose, understanding that learning can be facilitated and that learners do not need to be filled up with facts, acknowledgment of gender issues, and an experience of excitement about learning and life.

REFERENCES

Bateson, G., & Bateson, M. (1988). *Angels fear: Toward an epistemology of the sacred* (chap. 3). Retrieved on October 28, 2003, from http://www.oikos.org/angelsmetalogue.htm

Cleary, T. (1991) *Wen-tzu: Understanding the mysteries: Further teaching of Lao-tzu* (T. Cleary, Trans.). Boston: Shambhala.

Cohen, A. (1996a). *The purpose and value of group process in the life force seminars process-directed counselling training program.* Vancouver, BC, Canada: Life Force.

Cohen, A. (1996b). *The life force seminars process-directed counselling training manual.* Vancouver, BC, Canada: Life Force.

Cohen, A. (2002). The secret of effective psychotherapy: Metaskills. *The Private Practitioner Bulletin of the Canadian Counselling Association, 1,* 3.

Cohen, A. (2003). Process-directed group work approach. In S. Fehr, *Introduction to group therapy: A practical guide* (2nd ed., pp. 141–144). Binghamton, NY: Haworth Press.

Cohen, A. (2004). Multi-dimensional communication construction in the moment. *Insights: News for Clinical Counsellors, 15,* 12–13, 31–32.

Frankl, V. (1985). *Man's search for meaning.* New York: Washington Square Press.

Fehr, S. (2003). *Introduction to group therapy: A practical guide* (2nd ed.). Binghamton, NY: Haworth Press.

Jones, M. (1968). *Beyond the therapeutic community.* Montreal, QC, Canada: McGill University Press.

Jung, C. G. (1989). *Memories, dreams, and reflections* (R. Winston & C. Winston, Trans.). New York: Vintage Books, A Division of Random House, Inc.

Kubler-Ross, E. (1969). *On death and dying*. New York: MacMillan.

Leggo, C. (1998). Living un/grammatically in a grammatical world: The pedagogic world of teachers and students. *Interchange, 29*(2), 169–184.

Miller, J. P. (1993). *The holistic teacher*. Toronto, ON, Canada: OISE.

Mindell, Amy. (1995). *Metaskills: The spiritual art of therapy*. Tempe, AZ: New Falcon.

Mindell, Arnold. (1988). *City shadows: Psychological interventions in psychiatry*. New York: Routledge.

Mindell, Arnold. (1992). *The leader as martial artist: Techniques and strategies for resolving conflict and creating community*. New York: HarperCollins.

Mindell, Arnold. (1995). *Sitting in the fire: Large group transformation using conflict and diversity*. Portland, OR: Lao Tse Press.

Mindell, Arnold. (2002). *The deep democracy of open forums: Practical steps to conflict prevention and resolution for the family, workplace, and world*. Charlottesville, VA: Hampton Roads.

Palmer, P. J. (1998). *The courage to teach: Exploring the inner landscape of a teacher's life*. New York: Jossey-Bass/John Wiley & Sons.

Perls, F., Hefferline, R., & Goodman, P. (1951). *Gestalt therapy: Excitement and growth in the human personality*. New York: Dell.

Pierce, K. A., & Baldwin, C. (1990). Participation versus privacy in the training of group counsellors. *The Journal for Specialists in Group Work, 15*(3), 149–158.

Yalom, I. (1995). *The theory and practice of group psychotherapy* (4th ed.). New York: HarperCollins.

CHAPTER 5

WHO'S DIFFERENT,
WHO'S THE SAME?[13]

I saw, too, that my willingness to crucify myself on dark impulses and emotions distinguishes me from the criminal, who merely acts on them.

—Dallett (1991, p. 11)

I want it to be clear that emotion is not what is sacrificed, but rather the acting out of godlike power. It is crucial not to repress or deny emotion, but to endure it until it changes in its own way.

—Dallett (1991, p. 120)

The following essay, while having a very specific focus, speaks to the general tendency to marginalize and pathologize those who are different and describes the dilemmas inherent in classifying humans by category, demonstrates the importance of seeing each individual as unique, and illuminates the creative use of relationship and process orientation. Possibilities are suggested about how to relate to troubling, troubled, and "different" students, even though the paper is not specifically located in an educational environment. The labeling process is contested, and an argument is made for the importance of seeing the human being within the context of their life experience. This extreme example of what can happen with human beings affords an opportunity to look at persons who are far outside the mainstream and offers some ideas about what might be required and helpful in terms of perspective to recognize the diversity and uniqueness of any individual in a classroom. Some specific suggestions are offered about ways of being with those who may stand out more than others as different.

DISSOCIATIVE IDENTITY DISORDER: PERSPECTIVES AND ALTERNATIVES

> Ku-Shan was asked, "What is the basic object of investigation?"
>
> He replied, "How one has gotten to such a state."
>
> —Cleary (1998, p. 43)

So-called dissociative identity disorder (DID) is characterized by the manifestation of two or more separate and seemingly independent identities that may or may not be acknowledged by the individual within whom they reside. DID is described as a complex of experiences that occur in certain individuals who experience extreme abuse, neglect, or both, with associated emotional deprivation as children. A fact that is often overlooked in evaluating the history of a person who manifests extreme experiences such as DID is that early childhood experiences of neglect and abuse are not the core of the problem. The core is what this abuse and neglect replaces, which is proper bonding, love, and attention. These deficits are consistent features in children and adults with extreme behavioral manifestations, of which DID is an excellent example. Sakheim (1995) chronicles the relationship between DID and experiences of possession, ritual abuse, and trauma. In DID there is a history of trauma, extreme states (Arnold Mindell, 1988), and apparent dissociation into a number of identities within one individual. Usually, some of these identities claim to know about each other, and others do not. One person with whom I have worked for over a decade has lived in one identity that seems to be core for several years now, aside from one notable regressive experience during this time. She has told me that while she has full recall of her experiences as each part now, she claims that at the time she did not know her experience other than as each part separately—some of whom knew about each other, some who did not, some who knew who I was, and some who did not. It could be debated as to whether this is a truthful accounting of experience or not; what is not questionable is that I witnessed a person who was in an extreme state very frequently and who performed her life in many different roles. There were certainly times when I questioned what I was witnessing. What I was certain about was that I had witnessed a singular body that manifested many identities, either consciously or unconsciously. If I take this person at her word, then, in fact, the segregated experience was occurring. If this person was fabricating the experiences and it was all a gigantic pretense, at the least one would have to wonder what would compel a person to perpetuate such an elaborate performance over a period of years. Clearly there was a huge problem even if the segregated identity experiences were intended inventions. The suicidal gestures, accidents, disappearances, multiplicity of dwellings and relationships, and changes of costume and voice were actual verifiable experiences.

As I have outlined previously there are verifiable dimensions that accompany a person who seems to be manifesting more than one identity. There has been ongoing controversy as to whether this disorder even exists. Merskey (1995) contends that it does not and argues that the diagnosis itself interferes with optimal treatment. I would contend that the issue of diagnosis is problematic in itself as this suggests some repeatable and verifiable list of symptoms, and I would also say further that the idea of treatment is misplaced. The meaning of the word *diagnosis* provides some insight:

> **Diagnosis 1. a.** the process of determining by medical examination the nature and circumstances of diseased condition. **b.** the decision reached from such an examination. **2.** an analysis of the cause

or nature of a situation. **3.** an answer or solution to a problematic situation. (Random House, 1998)

The definition of the word, in fact, calls into question the entire procedure of diagnosis in the realm of the personal and interpersonal. However, my interest here is in the DID diagnosis. Calling this cluster of experiences a disorder suggests some kind of verifiable pathology that has its basis in something that is malfunctioning within the person. As is evident, conversation has to be deemed to constitute a "medical examination" and the accumulation of certain behaviors and experiences has to meet standards of quantity and time that are deemed sufficient to merit the diagnostic label. This process also assumes that the medical person performing the examination is objective and able to accurately discern the symptoms and that the patient is able to report accurately, as part of the diagnostic criteria involves the patient's ability to understand what is asked for and to report accurately. In the case of a DID diagnosis, presumably the clinical evidence is based on the ability of the practitioner to discern what may well be hidden from himself or herself and the patient. I believe that the question that must be raised is whether the description of emotional pain and the individual's attempts to resolve such pain really constitutes a medical diagnosis or is merely a moral label. Is what someone does the same as what someone has? Are broken hearts the same as hearts that are broken?

Another serious problem with the diagnostic category is that it perpetuates the core issue of these individuals. It essentially states that the person has a disorder, and there is no connection to background experiences. This reinforces the feelings of isolation and extreme loneliness that these individuals always demonstrate and, at times, talk about directly. The message is essentially that he or she is different and that something is going on over which he or she has no control and over which he or she never will have control. As these individuals feel no control over their experiences and they feel isolated, the diagnosis essentially incarcerates them in their experience. They are captured by diagnostic language. Alternatively, they can resist the diagnosis and risk being labeled as "in denial," another no-win situation, which is a re-creation of that with which they have always lived.

The evidence of developmental and bonding insults and ruptures is overwhelming with individuals who are diagnosed with DID. There are actual phenomena that indicate the ruptures, although this information may be very hard to come by. What is usually very apparent is that the person is experiencing immense difficulties. A response to the issue of whether the diagnosis exists or not is given by Lawler-Fahey (1995):

> Instead of arguing over the existence of multiple personality disorder or dissociation, we should recognize that dissociation exists in different degrees and continue to treat the victim, who is traumatized, rather than leave [him or her] without treatment while we argue over the validity of the diagnosis. (pp. 33–34)

While I like Lawler-Fahey's practicality, I do, as I stated previously, have problems with the word *treatment*. The word suggests that there is a disease or disorder. My experience with individuals manifesting different personalities is that there is always a history of extreme trauma and neglect in their background. I have worked with some individuals who are manifesting a number of personalities, and I would have to say that something is certainly going on. I have looked into the face of someone with whom I had worked for a number of years and had them look at me, on more than one occasion, incredulously and say, "Who are you, and what makes you think that you can talk to me in this personal way?" I have no question that something substantial and extreme is happening. Even if it is all consciously perpetrated by these individuals, I believe that the overall reasons for this way of being lies in fractured lives based in ruptures of bonding and development. I believe that what is required is quite different from what is usually done for these individuals, and I will elaborate on this next.

SEGREGATED PERSONALITY EXPERIENCE

If there is to be a name to describe these types of experiences I would suggest that the term Segregated Personality Experience (SPE) is more illustrative of what actually takes place and less stigmatizing than the term dissociative identity disorder (DID). SPE should suggest nothing more than that there is an experience related to personality occurring that is segregated from another experience. The idea of segregation denotes separation, division, or both but does not suggest any judgment or diagnostic process. Also, the word *experience* has a very different connotation than the word *disorder*. Experience simply means that a person knows something is happening while disorder indicates that there is something wrong or deranged within the person who is having the experience, and the experience is evidence of this. The term *SPE* is meant to be descriptive, relative, and not definitive. The fact of describing rather than diagnosing removes the experience from the sometimes violent effects of the diagnostic paradigm. Placing the description in a relativistic context lessens the potential for freezing the individual within the walls of a diagnosis in his or her eyes and in the eyes of the caregiver. As the term *SPE* is not definitive, it has less potential to be used as a weapon of oppression against individuals who are having relatively extreme experiences. I will illustrate later in this essay that there is a good reason that is in the interests of the individual experiencing SPE's for caregivers and care receivers to think about this as a cluster of experiences rather than a disorder. I describe the existing concept of DID in the upcoming text. Then I explicate the less stigmatizing view that I have characterized as SPE along with alternative views and approaches to working with persons who are living out experiences that fall within the descriptive parameters of SPE.

HISTORY

I would like to give some background on so-called DID, or as it was previously called, multiple personality disorder (MPD). The experience itself has a lengthy history that, according to an article (anonymous, 1998), "A History of Dissociative Identity Disorder," dates back to the Paleolithic period where it showed up in cave paintings. This article also notes that the condition was declared "extinct" in 1943 (Greaves, 1993a, p. 351). According to Greaves (1993a, p. 355), Eberhardt Gmelin may have been the first to report a case of multiple personality. Greaves (1993b) also notes an account in the 18th century of "exchanged personality" (p. 361). Various observations are recorded around the same time in the United States. An early case, Mary Reynolds, (Putnam, 1989, p. 28) was the first to capture public attention after an article appeared in *Harper's News Monthly Magazine* in 1860. A number of cases were also reported by Pierre Janet around the turn of the century. Eventually the film, *The Three Faces of Eve*, publicized this type of condition. Around this time, although still controversial, the phenomena was more generally acknowledged and accepted by health care professionals.

ETIOLOGY

The appearance of DID in a child is invariably preceded by extreme experiences of abuse, neglect, and/or some traumatic event or events that are accompanied by gross inconsistencies and unpredictability of behavior and communication by significant adults. In some cases, an extreme traumatic event seems to be the final straw for a fragile child. These circumstances are characterized by a gross lack of attention to and neglect of the child's needs at the time of the event, which is a form of neglect that is consistent with the history preceding the event. Kluft et al. (1984, pp. 283–301) state that severe traumatization within family systems is the experience for the majority of patients. Although Kluft refers to a "majority" of patients, in fact, I did not expect to find any cases that lacked this feature in the literature that I reviewed and indeed I did not. Braun (1985) reports that out of 18 patients, all reported evidence, which indicated transgenerational incidence of MPD. This indicates that these children had parents who were not capable of providing adequate parenting and who themselves had parents who also were not capable of providing adequate parenting. DID clients generally have poor recall of childhood events and, in particular, those events that were extreme and traumatizing. These clients experience dissociation, which means that the memories of personal history are split up amongst parts or that the part that has the memories is not readily accessible. To put this in another way, dissociation is a reasonable response to what a child in the circumstances outlined previously has experienced. Of course, not every child who has such experiences manifests DID, but in my experience, every child who has such backgrounds of neglect and abuse will demonstrate some extreme disturbance.

Discriminations about the etiology of DID may be useful for research purposes. This does not alter the fact that each person having this type of experience is unique and that therapy must be designed to fit the particular individual. There is no doubt that these individuals come from extremely disturbed backgrounds which lack most or all characteristics which would lay the groundwork for healthy and normal development.

I will outline here a theoretical possibility about the background of such individuals. Their experience is readily characterized as the opposite of what would be reasonably hoped for to give a child a good and secure internal base for going forward in life. From the beginning, they will come into the world with a parent or parents who are compromised and challenged in their capacity to function in the world, develop intimate relationships, and pay sufficient attention to a child. On top of this, they will be masters at delivering messages of impossibility—messages that essentially put a child consistently into situations that no matter what choice they make, it will be wrong. A very small example that identifies the type of pattern about which I am speaking could go like this,

> Mother says to her 2-year-old daughter, "Come over here and give Mommy a kiss." The toddler walks over and kisses her mother. Mother pinches the child's cheek hard enough to produce a yelp and tears. Mother says, "I shouldn't have to ask you for a kiss. You should just come over and give it to me." The child continues to cry. Mother then says, "Mommy feels unhappy when she sees you cry. Stop making Mommy unhappy. Now come and give Mommy a kiss."

Imagine the stress that this creates within the psyche-soma of a child who knows only this from their earliest days. A child of this age has no ability to understand in a way that will ascribe to her mother the type of crazy-making that mother is creating. The child has several options, one of which is to begin to dissociate from the pain of the pinches and, more substantially, from the wound of being unloved. Eventually something has to give, and what gives is the child's capacity to develop a sense of self that is secure and consistent. No core sense of self is ever able to form. The best possibility is to form personalities or imaginary friends. It is a survival move and so could well be evaluated as a good strategy for continuing to exist. Eventually the person grows older, the endemic stress takes its toll, and there are huge events that are predictable occurrences that can be summarized as a highly partitioned life, including accidents, suicide attempts, torturous relationships, exhaustion, and so on.

A highly dubious possibility in my view is that there is a well-established sense of self that somehow forms in spite of the continuous and pressing lack of love and that a decision is made to pretend to be all these other people and to act as if they are separate entities not known to him or her. Further, the person is able to keep track of all this and maintain it in a way that keeps it hidden from most. If individuals had the capacity to focus for a period of many years and hold all this together, one would have to wonder why they would bother, since clearly they have a highly unusual capacity to lead parallel lives and to keep clear what role does what, when, with who, all the while making sure that there is no overlap that will lead to being found out. I do not see this as a realistic possibility. My professional experience indicates to me that in all these individuals, without exception, early and basic bonding and developmental experiences are compromised severely, relationships are characterized by desperation, and life is lived in isolation and terror.

DSM-IVR Diagnostic Criteria

The *DSM-IVR* (American Psychological Association, 1994) describes the following diagnostic criteria for 300.14, dissociative identity disorder:

A. The presence of two or more distinct identities or personality states (each with its own relatively enduring pattern of perceiving, relating to, and thinking about the environment and self).

B. At least two of these identities or personality states recurrently take control of the person's behaviour.
C. Inability to recall important personal information that is too extensive to be explained by ordinary forgetfulness.
D. The disturbance is not due to the direct physiological effects of a substance (e.g., blackouts, or chaotic behaviour during Alcohol Intoxication) or a general medical condition (e.g., complex partial seizures).

Note: In children, the symptoms are not attributable to imaginary playmates or other fantasy play. (pp. 484–487)

Kluft (1985) reports the following case, which I cite here, as an example of the application of the diagnostic criteria:

> This 9-year-old boy was suicidal. He had a history of chaotic and disruptive behaviour. Clinicians had noted frequent behaviour suggesting a trance-like state. Two styles of behaviour were noted. In the first, he was depressed, lethargic and often dazed; in the second, he was aggressive, vigorous, alert, and always in trouble. In the first, he was partially amnesic for his behaviour; but in the second, he recalled all actions of the first. Each was different in voice, speech patterns, and movement characteristics. The first bore his current legal name. The second bore the name with which he was born—his father's name. The boy was three years old when his father died. Shortly thereafter, his mother had changed his name. (pp. 182–183)

This boy tentatively meets the criteria as outlined.

A. There are two distinct identities.
B. They both take control of his behavior.
C. He demonstrates inability to recall important information which is beyond what can be explained by ordinary forgetfulness.
D. There is no notation of any medical condition. This criterion is not met by way of this case description because there is no definitive statement ruling out a medical condition. There is no mention

of imaginary playmates—a criterion specific to children—which, if present, might rule a diagnosis of DID out.

Interestingly, DID is unique amongst extreme *DSM-IVR* diagnoses in that there is no recommendation for medication as a treatment protocol unless there is a dual diagnosis, that is, the DID diagnosis is combined with another diagnosis. The additional diagnosis would normally be deemed amenable to pharmaceutical treatment. I believe that the lack of drug therapy for DID is related to the lack of sufficient numbers of patients available with the diagnosis, and this makes drug research unprofitable.

SYMPTOMS

According to the *Guidelines for Treating Dissociative Identity Disorder (Multiple Personality Disorder) in Adults* (1997), the following symptoms may be present and should be explored: episodes of amnesia, fugue, depersonalization, derealization, identity confusion, identity alteration, age regressions, auto-hypnotic experiences, and hearing voices. Lewis (1996) notes:

> The characteristics of different personality states in children may be less fixed and well defined than in adult patients. What is more, their appearance and disappearance are often fleeting and therefore difficult to recognize...The clinician must keep in mind that DID/MPD is a secret disorder, hidden from the child as well as the clinician. (p. 304)

He also states, "The three core symptoms of DID/MPD are lapses of awareness, amnesias for events that occur during these lapses, and switches into alternate personality or behavioural states. These kinds of symptoms wreak havoc with academic and social functioning" (p. 305). There are a whole range of symptoms and behaviors that may only become evident when a sufficient level of trust and relationship is established with the therapist. Lewis (1996) identifies a long list of symptoms, including the following:

> command hallucinations, voices arguing with each other, headaches, rapid mood changes, trance-like states, unpredictability, restlessness, difficulty concentrating, impaired memory for learning material, suicidal behaviours, apparently lying, and apparently stealing. DID is often confused with other conditions. Clues such as differences in handwriting, denial of what is obvious to the external observer, changes in voice, changes which seem to indicate age shifts, sudden shifts in personality, having a part identify itself are all important indicators of the possibility of DID. (p. 310)

Lewis writes from the diagnostic paradigm. He refers to DID as a condition. As I have already discussed, identification of the experience as a discrete condition constructs a problem itself that compounds the already-existing problems.

THE EXPERIENCE

In this section I will attempt to put a little flesh on the bones of what the *DSM* criteria attempt to address. A person who has created the identities we call DID lives in a world within which he or she is very isolated. Each separate identity has a personality, history, relationship life, and behavioral patterns. Some identities may be just fragments and appear only for a brief time to fulfill a specific need or function. Some identities may be aware of other identities and have shared histories. Other identities may know everything and yet still be separate. Still, other identities are unaware of any other identities and will regard anyone who mentions other identities as crazy. The separate personalities develop as a response to extreme stress and may also appear in the moment in response to situations which may be physically, emotionally, or cognitively painful, incomprehensible, and intolerable. It is initially a way for a child to survive what is experienced as an excruciating situation. The child is not aware of the shifts and no one else notices, and this strategy is adopted and eventually becomes a way of life that continues on into adulthood.

The potential for DID is laid down from a very early point in life when the child can no longer cope. At this point, the split into discrete personalities begins. When children experiencing DID are brought into a treatment situation, just the fact of safety and removal from the noxious environment may have a salutary effect, although this in itself is not sufficient to prevent a return to the DID way of being when sufficient stressors are present. A person who has been assigned the DID label may be carrying on several different, more or less, complete lives. The person may have more than one job, more than one residence, several bank accounts, and different names and identification to go with each identity. Different identities develop to cope with different situations. Often these identities are in conflict with each other. One identity may be trying to look after itself while another is screaming orders which are extremely destructive.

The following dialogue demonstrates a typical interaction in working with a client experiencing DID: One morning I answered the phone in my office and heard a familiar voice. A voice that sounded like a young girl was saying, "Hi, it's Jeannie." A second later I hear another older and harsher voice, "That little bitch ought to be shot!" I recognized the voice of Janet, a part who had a very punitive attitude toward all the child parts. Then Jeannie was back. "I want to tell you what happened last night. Do you want to know? Do you have time? I don't want to interrupt your work, and I know it is almost your snack time." Jeannie knew my schedule and had made a note of my routines. I said, "It's okay. I'll have my snack while we talk. Tell me what happened." Jeannie started, "Well, we all woke up and went downtown at 3 a.m., and I was tired and I didn't want to go, but Joanne was being so stupid and saying we had to go." Right on cue I heard, "Hi! That little kid is such a pain. I told her she could sleep, but no, she had to see what was going on. She almost ruined everything. I wanted to meet Bob and get drunk, and she kept popping out and saying stupid things, like "can I have a cup of cocoa?" I laughed. Jeannie reappears. "What's wrong with having cocoa? I like cocoa." Joanne reappeared, "Can't you do something. You're the adult. She listens to you. Make her go to bed at 8. She's only 7. Can't you do something?" Janet popped out, "I hate these late nights. I'm exhausted. I don't think this is working. My life isn't working. I've got bandages on my wrists. I'm not sure how they got there. I think I cut myself. Can you come over here? I think I need to go to the hospital." The demand on me to switch between relationships rapidly, maintain and develop the relationships, be alert to danger, remember all the relationship dynamics between the parts, broker deals between parts, respond to requests for help, and generally hold a very leaky container together is very high.

A typical lifestyle of a DID person might look like the following: Three adult personalities with two separate residences and a day job and a night job—one job highly skilled such as a lawyer and the other as a night clerk in a skid row hotel. The third identity could share the residence of one of the "workers" and be a person who supposedly sleeps a lot and is lazy. The person might own two vehicles and have three separate sets of friends. It may be that there is a core contact person who has a sense of what is actually going on that the DID person keeps more or less in touch with as a security anchor, but even this person will be lacking large parts of the whole picture. There will likely also be child parts that require various degrees of attention. Older child parts will have their set of friends and interests. One identity might have a number of physical problems while other identities have no symptoms whatsoever. Some identities will show symptoms of great fatigue, which is reasonable given that the person is often getting little sleep. Accidents are a very recurrent feature of life, which is not surprising given the accumulated level of fatigue and stress and the lack of knowledge as to what is the reason for this fatigue and stress.

As documented by Murphy (1993, pp. 242–245), persons with a DID diagnosis have shown a remarkable ability to control physiological functioning. Cases have been cited of extremely rapid healing, and other cases have been reported where in one identity a person has an illness, and in another they do not. He suggests that in order to survive, persons with DID have maintained the lability and fluidity of early childhood as a survival mechanism and carry this ability into adulthood. This makes good sense in terms of viewing DID developmentally. I would suggest that there is an extreme developmental breakdown in the first 3 years of a child's life. This breakdown is compounded as the child grows up due to an inherent dissociative capacity in combination with an ongoing complex of factors comprising abuse and neglect that mitigate in favor of DID as a response.

I contend that the evidence as I have outlined to this point makes the case that DID is not a disorder but a cluster of extreme responses to overwhelmingly unfavorable circumstances. If this is the case, then the idea that DID is a discrete entity and a disorder to be treated is wrong and leads to a treatment of something that does not exist. At best, the treatment will be helpful in spite of the incorrect view. It will be helpful for reasons related to relationship and care extended by the therapist. At worst, insistence on the diagnosis will recreate the original situation where the person was treated like an object and not as a vulnerable child, and the damage will be bolstered and furthered.

TREATMENT MODELS FOR DID/SPE

Ross (1995) outlines his view of the proper treatment approach to DID. The characteristics of this treatment include the following:

> ...The therapist is not a friend of the client, therapist and client are not on a mutual spiritual journey, they are not involved in each other's personal lives outside of therapy, and the purpose of the treatment is not re-parenting. The therapist cannot fill up the emptiness inside the client through indiscriminate 'caring.' (p. 414)

Ross views more than 3 hours of therapy per week as regressive and as fostering dependency on the therapist. He suggests that cognitive approaches are most efficacious and that the goals are symptom reduction and improvement in psychosocial function. This view is dangerous as it completely denies the reality that these individuals have deep, unresolved dependency needs that are an outcome of extremely impaired early bonding and attachment experience and that there is a requirement for a complex, process-oriented, highly individualized approach in order to begin to address the dilemma of SPE. Any approach that does not include acknowledgment of these attachment challenges will reproduce and reinforce the original struggle for survival for the person and really says more about the therapist's fears of dependency.

Putnam's (1989) view outlines eight stages in the treatment of DID: making the diagnosis, initial interventions, initial stabilizations, acceptance of the diagnosis, development of communication and cooperation, metabolism of the trauma, resolution and integration, and development of post-resolution coping skills. While I disagree with Putnam's framing and his conception of diagnosis, I endorse the attention he recommends to the intra and inter psychic dimensions that he outlines. Attention to these domains is central to work with these individuals. Referring to these dimensions of the therapy as stages is misleading, as this implies a sequential process. This is not reflective of the actual experience with individuals who are living with dissociative events and who have periods where they are more present and periods that are regressive.

FUTURE RESEARCH IDEAS

There is a complexity of issues which predisposes an individual to develop DID as opposed to other conditions. The predisposition for dissociation has been identified. There do not seem to be any indicators for what creates this predisposition. There is potential for research in the areas of family of origin, unresolved deaths and losses, birth order, predisposing physiology and the interaction of genetics, cellular biology, psychology, and intelligence to name a few areas that have potential for exploration.

Individuals with SPE very frequently have a history of abuse that involves their body. The capacity to tolerate body sensation is extremely compromised. The response to uncomfortable or unexpected body sensation is to shift to a personality that does not feel the sensation. The same holds true for the feeling of emotion. The area of body sensation and emotion is fertile ground for research.

A very useful idea for therapists working with individuals experiencing SPE is the concept of metaskills. Amy Mindell (1995) defines metaskills as the in-the-moment feelings and attitudes of the therapist that are reflective of deeply held values and beliefs. Her observations about metaskills derived from her curiosity as to why therapists from a variety of orientations seemed to be successful. She wondered what, if anything, they held in common. Her research demonstrated that while they all professed different theoretical frames of reference, what they had in common was a range and depth of metaskills. From this, she concluded that metaskills were more significant in terms of a positive outcome than the theoretical framework of the therapist. I have no question that therapists working with extreme states (Arnold Mindell, 1988) such as SPE must have a wide repertoire of metaskills.

ALTERNATIVE APPROACHES

Individuals dealing with SPE are stuck at a very early stage of development. They appear to have developed a number of personality constructs for survival purposes. They live in a more or less constant state of existential despair and angst. Initially and during regressive phases, the therapy process involves basic care more than what is usually viewed as psychotherapy. Relationships need to be developed with each part, and there must be a continuing emphasis on self-care, which includes what I have called the three basics—nutrition, rest, and exercise. Individuals who experience SPE do not, nor are they able to, attend to any of these dimensions of self-care in any regular systematic way. A secondary purpose of this emphasis on basics is the establishment of routine and structure into what has invariably been an exceedingly chaotic lifestyle. During this time, the therapist is establishing a connection with as many parts as possible, finding out the nature of each of the personalities, and facilitating the individual to become familiar with their own experience.

It is important to remember that the individual with SPE is desperate and that there is no way that this will be a usual therapy relationship. At times, it may seem more like doing group therapy than individual therapy. Often the only thing that really matters is keeping this individual alive and enlisting and aligning with the parts that want to help. It is essential to strategically support the autonomy of a part who is acting independently in a constructive way, but somewhat like a parent, the therapist must warn of potential danger.

Therapy with SPE individuals is usually measured in years and even decades. These people have been shattered and always at a developmental point where experiences of wholeness were limited and unconscious. The recovery process is long and torturous. Personality parts ought to be identified as symptomatic responses to stressors. At some point, the individual may begin to rely on the therapist to advise them and can eventually begin to identify these stressors themselves and deal with them by staying with sensation and/or feelings or by avoiding the stressful situation. This will constitute a major shift from the previous pattern of shifting into an alternative personality to avoid feeling emotions and physical sensations. These individuals have a very limited capacity to deal with uncomfortable feelings, and they also have difficulty separating the demands and feelings of others from their internal experience. Over time they can learn to contain an uncomfortable feeling and to differentiate more clearly between themselves and others. For persons with SPE, chaos is a usual state of affairs, and they may have difficulty adapting to what they experience as boring when they are no longer moving from crisis to crisis. The collaborative task is to learn to live in states of relative peace and quiet.

When a relatively well-established alliance has developed, dissociation into parts is a much less frequent experience and the person will be able to begin to understand what has happened to them, who they are, the meaning of their experience, how to deal with their life, and what it is they want to do.

In my view the only ethical possibility in working with individuals who are having SPE involves integration of the parts into a whole and recovery of full consciousness for the individual. I suggest that if the view of segregated personalities as reflective of the outcome of an early and continuous bonding rupture is accepted, along with the associated segregation experience in consciousness, then recovery of wholeness is clearly the goal of the process. The person is living in a series of bubbles, which for them are impermeable, and in parts of their experience unknown. The responsibility of the therapist is to carry the often very heavy burden of the connections and history of the person and to share these experiences with various parts and the core part as opportunity presents itself. A key dilemma for these individuals is the lack of a meta-communicator (Arnold Mindell, 1988). A person who lacks the capacity of this dimension is not able to communicate about experience. Persons in extreme states (Arnold Mindell, 1988) over time and as their awareness, self-care, and ability to relax and handle emotions and sensations slowly develops demonstrate a decreased tendency to segregate. Over time he or she becomes aware of the continuum of experience that can lead to segregation experience. It is crucial for the therapist to support the development of awareness and to fill in whenever the person is not able to do so. The appearance of a metacommunicator function is a sign that there is integration occurring. The person demonstrates an increasing ability to notice foreground and background processes. For these people, the option to not be *self aware* is not an option if he or she wants to live without segregation or dissociation. The therapist's task is to do what is required, that is, to hold the skein of reality when the person cannot and to pass over this task as much as possible as the person becomes more capable of being an integrated being.

THERAPIST ALERTNESS IS ESSENTIAL

It is crucial that therapists see and accept what is presented by these individuals. "Accepting" means not denying what is occurring and seeing it for what it is. It does not mean accepting that this is the way it is supposed to be and that this is okay.

One of my earliest SPE events involved receiving a phone call from a 25-year-old female client whom I had been seeing for about 3 months. The voice was familiar but sounded different—younger. The situation she described seemed a little odd and out of the context with which I was familiar in my previous work with Belinda. Something was alerted inside me, and I found myself asking, "What's your name?" The answer was chilling in its simplicity, "Bonnie." I went a little further, "How old are you?" The response was again surprising and informative, "Six." The important dimension was that I noticed the clues and pursued their meaning. I had enough previous experience with this client where she had been vague and seemingly forgetful that I felt that a direct question about the changes would not be useful.

On another occasion, a therapist who was seeing me for consultation told me about a client that she was seeing who was very troubling to her. She described situations where her client, a young woman, seemed to go into trance-like states and other situations where she had great difficulty ending the sessions as her client seemed to be immobilized. She noticed her countertransference that included thoughts suggesting that she ought to look after this woman by taking her home with her. She described experiences where she felt her only option was to walk her client out to the parking lot to her car only to find that the woman seemed to have difficulty recognizing her vehicle and also seemed vague as to what to do when she got into it. The therapist also observed that her client would often get into her car and not go anywhere for extended periods of time. I suggested that she ask some questions about name and age. In our next meeting, she reported responses that confirmed SPE.

On another occasion, I was conducting a workshop for therapists. I asked for a volunteer so I could demonstrate working with resistance by cooperating with the person who is resistant. I explained that my view of resistance is that it is just another way of responding—one I may not expect. I wanted to demonstrate various ways of going with the person who was being contrary rather than the more common approaches of interpretation and working through. A woman volunteered gleefully when I framed my request somewhat humorously by asking for someone who was feeling especially difficult and ornery that day. We engaged in a dialogue, and she immediately began to demonstrate her contrariness. I said, "How are you feeling being up here in front of the group?" She responded loudly and with a big smile on her face, "None of your business!" I said, "You're right, and you needn't tell me anything that you don't want to." She looked a little surprised, and said, "Really, do you mean it?" I said, "Yes." She went on, "I don't trust you." I replied, "Who says you should."

Again her face showed some change. I noticed a change in her demeanor. She volunteered a surprising statement in a voice that was younger sounding, "I like you. My name is Jamie. I am 7. I'm a hungry boy. Can I have something to eat?" Apparently her contrary and belligerent style was a defense for her that served to contain her segregated personality parts. My cooperation and joining with her had the quick effect of bringing out what was hidden. Three other parts emerged in quick succession. The demonstration was over in 15 minutes. I was concerned as the demonstration had certainly gone further than I had envisioned. She went back to her main personality looking a little stressed. She seemed to have an idea as to what had occurred, and she made a comment that "I hope no one thinks I am a multiple personality." I was even more concerned when during the discussion and question period, no one in the group of 20 therapists asked about what had occurred nor did anyone ask me about it afterward. All the comments and questions were about how to cooperate with resistance. It was as if no one had seen what had occurred.

There is a tendency to deny and marginalize what is unfamiliar, and therapists are not immune to this. I recommend that small and particularly recurring anomalies be pursued with clients. Simple inquiries can lead to very revealing disclosures. At worst, the therapist will be asked why he or she is asking such an odd question and may have to deal with some feelings of embarrassment. I would suggest that a prime directive is to acknowledge to yourself what is actually occurring in front of you. This is valuable with any client and particularly with those having SPE.

ANECDOTES ABOUT THE EXPERIENCE

A general commentary from those who have more or less come out of the SPE experience and lead a more integrated life is that there is some truth to the idea that the experience is not what it may seem to be and yet that the experiences exist. The descriptions suggest that the person comes from a background of extreme bonding ruptures from the earliest stages of life and that these ruptures are characterized by impossible double-bind type messages. The person grows up knowing little, if any, real attention, particularly, attention always comes with a high emotional cost. At some point, it becomes apparent that the pain is too much to bear and that the way to get attention and not feel hurt is to switch into a role that will hold the interest and attention of another person. As well, the SPE person in a subidentity cannot be hurt much by any failure in the attempt to get the needed attention. The SPE person is very frequently exhausted and yet still pushing to get more of that which they can never get enough attention and love without conditions. The roles have an automaticity to them, and yet there is a curious sense of watching from within that over which they feel no control and for which they have no language. When the stress and fear reach maximums, the person will begin to manifest fragments of personalities that have very short half-lives and who essentially perform functions and will act as if they do not know people who previously have been significant and who are in touch sufficiently, such as a therapist. In fact, they are exhausted. In some sense, the word *dissociation* applies well, but it is not just a cognitive experience—it is holistic and not separated from the physical components and the effects of personal history.

CONCLUSION

In work with SPE individuals the therapist must have access to a wide range of metaskills, including flexibility, fluidity, compassion, and patience. The therapist must have a great tolerance for being in processes of not-knowing and ambiguity. The ability to think on one's feet is essential to facilitate the development of the multiplicity of relationships, communication between parts, and steadying. Quickness and fluidity is sometimes necessary as all this may need to be done within the space of a few minutes. Most importantly, the therapist must be interested in and skilled with work on their inner life (Cohen, 2004). It is not possible to work with these individuals without having your own inner processes activated. It is a remarkable personal growth opportunity. The therapist will have many extreme experiences of a double-bind nature and will have the privilege and the torment of entering into a very unusual world characterized by extreme states of consciousness.

References

American Psychiatric Association. (1994). *Diagnostic and statistical manual of mental disorders* (4th ed.). Washington, DC: Author.

Anonymous. (1998). *A history of dissociative identity disorder*. Retrieved on July 10, 2004, from http://www.siri.net/~whisper/insideout/dd/history.htm

Braun, B. (1985). The transgenerational incidence of dissociation and multiple personality disorder: A preliminary report. In P. Kluft (Ed.), *Childhood antecedents of multiple personality*. Washington, DC: American Psychiatric Press.

Cleary, T. (1998). *Teachings of Zen*. (T. Cleary, Trans.) Boston: Shambhala.

Cohen, A. (2004) *Contemplations on and rumors about the inner life of the educator: Inner experiences as data for conversion into practice and practice as catalyst for inner experience*. Unpublished manuscript, University of British Columbia, Vancouver, Canada.

Dallett, J. O. (1991). *Saturday's child: Encounters with the dark gods*. Toronto, ON, Canada: Inner City.

Greaves, G. (1993). *A history of multiple personality disorder*. New York: Putnam.

International Society for the Study of Dissociation. (1997). *Guidelines for treating dissociative identity disorder (multiple personality disorder) in adults*. Glenview, IL: International Society for the Study of Dissociation.

Kluft, R., Braun, B., & Sachs, R. (1984). Multiple personality, interfamilial abuse, and family psychiatry. *International Journal of Family Psychiatry, 5*, 283–301.

Kluft, R. (1985). *Childhood multiple personality disorder: Predictors, clinical findings, and treatment results: Childhood antecedents of multiple personality.* Washington, DC: American Psychiatric Press.

Kluft, R. (1995). Current controversies surrounding dissociative identity disorder. Northvale, NJ: Jason Aronson.

Lawler-Fahey, M. (1995). Correspondence: Reactions and replies. *British Journal of Psychiatry, 161,* 268–284.

Lewis, O. (1996, April). Diagnostic evaluation of the child with dissociative identity disorder/multiple personality disorder. *Child and Adolescent Psychiatric Clinics of North America, 5*(2), 303–331.

Merskey, H. (1995). The manufacture of personalities: The production of multiple personality disorder. *The British Journal of Psychiatry, 160,* 327–340.

Mindell, Amy. (1995). *Metaskills: The spiritual art of therapy.* Tempe, AZ: New Falcon.

Mindell, Arnold. (1988) *City shadows: Psychological interventions in psychiatry.* New York: Routledge.

Murphy, M. (1993). *The future of the body: Explorations into the further evolution of human nature.* New York: Putnam.

Putnam, F. W. (1989). *Diagnosis and treatment of multiple personality disorder.* New York: Guilford.

Random House Webster's College Dictionary (2nd ed.). (1998). Toronto, ON, Canada: Random House.

Ross, C. A. (1995). Current treatment of dissociative identity disorder. In L. Cohen, J. Berzoff & M. Elin (Eds.), *Dissociative identity disorder* (pp. 413–434). Northvale, NJ: Jason Aronson.

Sakheim, R. (1995). Allegations of ritual abuse. In L. Cohen, J. Berzoff, & M. Elin (Eds.), *Dissociative identity disorder.* Northvale, NJ: Jason Aronson.

CHAPTER 6

DREAMING LIFE: WORKING WITH A PERSONAL DREAM— ON MY OWN

[Process Work] begins with the stuff of everyday life: problems and preoccupations, delights, hopes, and dreams. ...everyday experiences hold worlds within themselves.... Process Work methods provide a...system of tracking, mapping, and unfolding the flow of momentary experience, or 'process.' [which] allows you to venture beyond the bounds of preconceived notions, familiar experience, and everyday identity and still find your way home. . . .

Mindell developed an awareness modality that went beyond the dichotomy of health and sickness. He coined the expression 'the dream happening in the moment' to convey the idea that a numinous background to everyday reality manifests continually and in a multitude of ways.

Process Work...acknowledges the world of night-time dreams and the 'dreaming' world long recognized by mystics and indigenous peoples. ...[And] the world that is generally perceived as 'real' in contemporary societies. Viewing experience with this kind of multileveled awareness...you can see parts of yourself that everyday consciousness normally keeps hidden from view. ...Process Work affirms your spontaneous, multifaceted, and diverse nature, encouraging it to unfold in its own way.

—Diamond and Spark-Jones (2004, pp. xi–xii)

This essay is an extended narrative of personal inner work. While it is based on a dream, the methods could be applied to any situation and include identification with dream parts; following the stream of my consciousness; discovery through writing; enrollment in the dream community, that is, those who hear my dream; interpretation; dialogue between dream parts; and discovery and analysis of meaning. It is included as a very specific example of inner work and its potential for personal and professional development.

In particular, in education the daily events would be in place of the dream content but can be seen as constituting a dream in memory. Inner work on these daily events, particularly ones that have some feeling for the educator, holds a key to greater self-knowledge and fluid classroom practice. I contend that education is influenced by the internal and unconscious frames of reference of educators, and so it is incumbent on educators to be in an ongoing process of looking into their own inner life. The potential effect of this inner work is to increase awareness as to what the constituents of the inner and unconscious world of the educator are and to mitigate against unconscious and undesirable influence and effect on students. This essay describes a process to transform inner experience and its outward expression into optimally authentic expression in classrooms.

The writing is framed as closely as possible to reflect the process and method of the inner work itself, came as an emergence from my unconscious, and was part of the discovery process itself. As I wrote, I felt that I was more a vehicle than an agent for the words, feelings, and ideas that emerged. I am meaning unconscious as described by Jung (1989), as a repository for everything that is unknown.

THE DREAM BEGINS

The sea that calls all things unto her calls me, and I must embark.

—Kahlil Gibran in *The Prophet* (2001, p. 9)

What follows in this essay is a personal dream that has stayed alive in my consciousness for over a decade and is a continuance of a lifetime of wondering whether I am dreaming life, life is dreaming me, or if life and I are facets of a whole struggling to recognize our unity. The essay is written intentionally but without premeditated strategy and in a way that I hope will demonstrate the ideas that I am describing both in form, content, and process. There is ambiguity of meaning, a lack of solutions and closure, and I hope a sense of how to access the dreaming process.

Work on my self on my own is a practice that I have developed over the course of my professional career as a psychotherapist and educator. I have three purposes in this essay:

1.   To demonstrate the process, method, and potential of work on self alone.
2.   To demonstrate the efficacy of writing in the service of this inner research.
3.   To share the work itself as a potential mirror for readers.

I will share the personal work, insights, meanings, and identity shifts that have emerged from this work. I will also share my conversations with various people within my *dream community*, those with whom I share the dream and who share their responses about my dream, their insights, and the effect of their responses on me.

The text contains personal disclosures. Since the work is personal, this seems to make sense, and I am also motivated by my belief that knowing something about the person that I am sheds light on the meaning of what I have written and would be true no matter what the topic. I believe that any understanding of a person's ideas is enhanced by knowing something about the author of those ideas. You may also say that the theme of this writing lends itself totally to these disclosures, and I would agree. Imagine, however, writing that includes some relevant information about the personal process of the author related to the topic and the writing of the essay. Do you think that would enhance a reader's understanding and insight into the topic? I believe that *Uncommon Wisdom: Conversations With Remarkable People* (Capra, 1988) supports this idea.

A dream is an event that is remembered, described in narrative form, emerges in consciousness during sleep, and is remembered when awake. As the dream unfolds, it is the only known reality I know. The term *dream* is applied in the waking state.

Arnold Mindell (2001) suggests that there is a connection between everyday life and the spiritual dimension. He contends that inner work on dreams, both waking and sleeping contains this possibility. He also says that dreams contain information about identity, its construction, and the conduct of everyday life. Finally, he states that without a knowing of the source of dreams we cannot properly understand them or who we are. He goes on to say that paying attention to small signals that are easily dismissed, not noticed, or marginalized such as these occurrences offers an entry opportunity into a deeper understanding of life.

According to Tulku (2000), who writes from the Tibetan Buddhist view of the origin of dreams; dreams are representations of imprints that have possible roots from any point in our existence. He describes three types that are apparent: "1. imprints which determine our concepts, which have a great impact on our apperception; 2. imprints which determine our feeling or emotion, i.e., our self-feeling and self or other reference; 3. imprints which determine the manifestation of appearances" (p. 273).

As you read on, you will see all three of these types of imprints are apparent in my descriptions and process of inner work. What is also described is how these imprints have played out in my consciousness and in my life experience. You will see how my work on the dream transforms the imprints and clarifies my consciousness, albeit not easily or quickly.

Tulku goes on to describe three strategies for dealing with conflict, threat, and/or fear in a dream. These strategies are integrated with his idea that what is threatened is the dreamer's identity.

1. *Flight.* In fleeing the aggressor, the dreamer then misses the opportunity to work with his weak identity. Instead, he again manifests his weaknesses.

2. *Fight.* The dreamer feels strengthened by fighting that which attacks his dream-subject identity.
3. *Surrender.* ...The dreamer can let the aggressor destroy his dream-subject, i.e., he can unite with the negativity. When the negativity destroys the dream-subject, it destroys that with which one identifies. (pp. 279–280)

As you will see, all three strategies are employed next and what becomes apparent is that the meanings of the different dream figures and objects are not simply one thing or another. The encounter with and integration of otherness is a central part of the inner work that I describe.

INNER WORK AND RESEARCH METHODOLOGY

While this essay describes inner work on a personal dream, it also demonstrates a research methodology. Most research is focused toward getting some result. This method is interested in the response to a particular open-ended question—What will happen if, or next, or?—that is asked in response to an ongoing sequence of events that are themselves often both questions and answers. The inner research that is being conducted and described below involves noticing events, responding to them, and following the path of my own consciousness and wondering in response to those events. The "outcome" is whatever the next step in the process is. My method is to discover what makes sense in the situation, as it is at the time in the context that includes me and whoever or whatever else is present. This approach is linked to heuristic research methods (Moustakas, 1988, 1990, 1994, 1995), process-oriented methods (Amy Mindell, 2002; Arnold Mindell, 1984/2000, 1985, 1990/2000, 2001), and Gestalt methods (Perls, 1947/1969, 1951).

As a researcher, I have tended to follow my own process, take the line of least resistance, not be too concerned about the reactions of others, and to follow my own inner experience in its interactive relationship with the world. Moustakas (1990) says:

> Heuristic processes relate back to the internal frame of reference. Whether the knowledge derived is attained through tacit, intuitive, or observed phenomena—whether the knowledge is deepened and extended through indwelling, focusing, self-searching, or dialogue with others—its medium or base is the internal frame of reference. (p. 26)

All research is influenced by the internal frame of reference of the researcher, and so the researcher must reflect on his or her own inner landscape. The potential effect of this inner work is to increase awareness as to what is in the researcher's inner and unconscious world and to mitigate against any potentially detrimental influence and effect of their inner world and an understanding of the inter-relationship between their inner world and the phenomena under study. For example, my inquiry into a variety of approaches to the art and craft of psychotherapy reveals an obvious alliance between the personal history of the theorist and the theory that he or she developed. Freud was a product of his times. Apparently, he didn't like to look people in the eye. Fritz Perls, the founder of Gestalt therapy, was trained as a psychoanalyst. He felt that this type of work was far too intellectual and, consequently, developed an approach that was much more active and with a focus on what was occurring in the here and now. I don't think this affinity is escapable in any research, but this does not make the research less rigorous or relevant. It does mean, however, that the importance of the researcher's inner world as a key dimension of the research undertaking must be comprehensively accounted for in the research findings.

I align with Arnold Mindell (2001), who said, "It is clear to me that dreams are just one of the manifestations of 'the unconscious'" (p. 9). Other manifestations are experiences in the body, in relationship, day dreams, movements, and perceptions of world events. In other words, I can learn about myself and life at any and every moment by exploring these experiences in the way that unfolds below.

The idea of "creative emergence" (Jones, 2004), which is described as "a process of transformation that occurs during a particular research project, through the application of Process Work skills and metaskills to obstacles in the researcher's path" (p. 6), captures the essence of my process in this essay. Jones describes how obstacles and difficulties become part of the researcher's research process by "valuing and believing in emergency as a threshold of possibility" (p. 7). The use of metaskills such as curiosity help the researcher navigate processes that are difficult in a way that will uncover their hidden message and to see these obstacles as potential allies rather than the more common view that these problems are to be avoided, gotten around, and despaired about. Metaskills (Cohen, 2002; Arnold Mindell, 2001) are described as the in-the-moment feelings and attitudes that are brought to bear and reflect the most deeply held values, beliefs, and sense of self of the researcher. The idea is to approach the difficulty as a creative opportunity using process-oriented methods and employing the appropriate metaskills.

Perls (1947/1969) describes "correct concentration" as "fascination" (p. 188). Everything that is not about the object of interest fades into the background. There is no effort made to concentrate. The natural curiosity of the person takes over and attends to the experience that is central. The difficult part is being able to actually allow an unfettered experience of this "concentration" to occur. This is the process of inner work as demonstrated in my work on this dream. The dream shows my unconscious and leads me toward expanded consciousness about myself and, consequently, frees me to be more present in the world.

THE DREAM

This is a mid-life dream. At age 12, in regular life, I did not yet have the dog that appeared in the dream. I use the present tense to bring the dream alive in this moment.

> I am in my front yard, which is not a yard with which I am actually familiar. My dog, Rocky, a Bedlington Terrier, is here also. I am aware that a bear is approaching. I can't see him. He is coming from the forest whose border is right

at the edge of our yard, and I just know that he is coming. I feel apprehensive. I call Rocky. I am very frightened. I am afraid for him and for myself. I am afraid of losing him. I am scrambling up the stairs, which are extraordinarily steep. I am struggling to get up the stairs. Rocky is doing what he often does. He is ignoring me. I am having difficulty ascending the stairs, and I am very frightened that he will be killed. I see the bear. He is a gigantic, blue, black Kodiak bear; at least 10 feet tall. Rocky is small. He has no sense of the danger and no fear. He rushes up to the bear, barking. He is making darting movements towards the bear. The bear looks off to some far distant place. He pays no attention to Rocky. I continue to call Rocky and struggle to climb the stairs to the safety of the house and the front door which I long to be on the other side of.

The bear comes from the forest. Rocky and I are at home! One animal creature comes from a natural environment. Two other living beings, me and my dog, come from a man made structure, a house, from civilized society. On the other hand a dog, any dog, has roots in the wild and that a part of him, as is apparent in the dream, is still not domesticated. He lives in both places and moves through the space between. The juxtaposition of place of emergence is, man made on one side and natural on the other.

My dream is full of space. The relationship between the living things is comprised of moving toward, running away, and running around. The three living things are in a contained space. All the action in my dream takes place in the front yard between the forest and my house, on the ground, and beneath the sky.

I cannot wait any longer nor can the bear or my dog. Forces are at work beneath the surface of my consciousness. Each of us is moving. The bear is moving toward me and Rocky. Rocky rushes toward the bear. I am moving physically away with difficulty, and emotionally, I am pulled toward the bear and Rocky. I am torn. I am torn. My tornness is an inner experience. I think I have always been torn.

SOME TERMINOLOGY

There are some terms that are important in looking at my dream. The term *state* means something that is, at least for some period of time, apparently not changing. I differentiate a state from the thoughts about the state. For example, I can be afraid. That is my state. It is also an emotion, but I am calling it a state here because of its persistence over time. I can say in some way to myself, "I don't like being afraid." This is a thought about my state. It is not the state itself. The term *process* indicates something that is moving, changing, and/or developing. As you will see, the events in my dream change. There is a process. What does not change for me much in the dream is my feeling state. My state represents a personal edge. The term *edge* refers to a limit in my ability to experience. It demonstrates that point beyond which I have no experience. My identity is at its limit. I do not have any knowledge of who I am beyond this state in these particular circumstances. The possibility explored here is the expansion of my conscious and my sense of who I am and the implications this may have for me, for those around me, and for what I can do. The metacommunicator (Arnold Mindell, 1990/1990) is the aspect of consciousness that observes and comments nonjudgmentally and is not participatory in the dream, at least not in the ways that Rocky, the bear, and little Avi are.

PROCESS OF THE DREAM

I know the bear is coming before he appears. I sense his presence. He is moving toward the house. I fear for my safety and for the safety of my dog. I am struggling to get to safety by climbing up. My dog runs toward the bear barking, arrives, and then runs around him. The bear is moving slowly. There are a number of vectored forces. My description is from an observer position, from my metacommunicator.

Dream Space

The physical atmosphere in the dream is visually clear. There is fear within me; aggression, in the sense of moving toward, which Rocky represents; and power, which the bear represents. I am trying to be farther away from the bear and behind a barrier—the door to my house. I am running from aggression and nobility. Simultaneously, my heart is drawn

toward Rocky and the bear. Rocky is trying to be as close as possible to
the bear. The bear is not in any apparent way relational with respect to
me or Rocky. Any relational response he has is not obvious. He matters
to us. I see no evidence that we matter to him or even that we don't.

Movement
I am struggling to move up and away from the bear and my dog. Rocky is
moving away from me and towards the bear. The bear is moving towards
me and Rocky physically and seemingly towards an unseen, unknown
destination. He is apparently doing this without reference to either of us.
At the same time as I move away, my heart is drawn toward the combination of the two animals.

Emotions and...
Fear, lack of fear, calmness, and love...I am fearful. Rocky is uncon-
cerned and energized. He is instinctual. The bear is above it all. He does
not seem to be affected by what is around him. At least if he is, there is
no external visual clue.

Inner Thoughts
>LITTLE AVI: I am scared!! I want Rocky to come. He won't.
>BEAR: No thoughts.
>ROCKY: No thoughts.

The animals are without thoughts. Are they in a higher state of consciousness, or are they just in an instinctual state? Perhaps both?

Dream Parts, Life, and Me
A method from Gestalt therapy is to become the part. This idea is also
part of Buddhist philosophy (Hahn, 1998), which suggests that, in fact
we are the other and the problem is a lack of recognition of this. Within
the Gestalt framework, the more fully I can assume this identity in the
moment, the more I can re-own the disowned aspects of myself that
are represented by the part. To fully identify with a part of a dream can

involve feeling, thoughts, sensation, movement, sound, and/or expression in words. It is like putting on a new item of clothing and finding out how it fits, how to alter it so it fits, or how to activate the part of me that will naturally grow into it.

Even though I appear in the dream, it is fair to say that the Little Avi in the dream is a disowned part of me that still requires integration.

> LITTLE AVI: I am frightened. I feel the fear in my body. I am moving. I do not feel ownership of my movement. The bear is the cause. I am running away. I feel like I am being moved away. I want to get into my house. My house is safety. I want my dog to come. He does not respond to my call. He runs toward the bear. I am terrified. Rocky, Rocky, come here! Here Rocky! Here Rocky! Rocky! Rocky! I feel helpless. I am afraid he will be killed. I love my dog. I cannot protect him. He is so small, and Bear is so big. I cannot stop what is happening. I am struggling to get up these very steep stairs.

Let me now introduce to you a representation of some of you. I will call this person Every Reader (ER).

> ER: What is this monologue about? How do you do this? What's it for? Can I do this with my dreams?
>
> AVRAHAM: In this monologue, I have become dream Avi—little Avi. I take on this identity in the service of understanding what I see as my dream projection that is represented by little Avi. I want as much as possible to become this part in the service of understanding who I am and who the frightened child that still exists within me is. I want to establish a connection with this part of myself. I use the behavior as a route into the identity of the person who performs the behavior. I want to know who this person is. Change will emerge from connection and not out of a forced effort to change.
>
> My dog is instinctual. If he represents my instinct, then my feeling and attitude toward it is clear. I am not identified with it. In fact, I am separated from it, but not completely. I see it and am fearful of what may result from its being exercised. There are many things missing in my dream, as in all dreams.

What is significant is what stands out to me as missing—joy (mine) and connection to instinct. Yet all these dimensions are in the dream and beckoning to me to join with them.

ROCKY: I hear nothing. I will run toward this thing. My doing and being are one. I am exactly what I am. I am instinct. I am ecstatic like the dervish Azeem—the mighty one.

BEAR: I am beyond all things. I see within and without. The words do not begin to convey what I know. The spaces between the words say more. The spaces between and within me are full of emptiness that is pregnant with possibility.

The bear says that emptiness is important. He alludes to the unseen and empty that implies something full of potential. Standing on the edge of a precipice, the space between the edge and the ground represents many possibilities including death, beauty, and flight.

Relationships

LITTLE AVI: I call Rocky. He does not respond. I am terrified of the bear. He is big. I am not. I want to get away from him so he cannot hurt me. I am moving away. I want Rocky closer to me so he will be safe.

This seems like a normal desire, but in dreams, things are very often not as they appear. I want to have a relationship with the bear that includes a barrier, which makes sense if the bear is a bear. It also makes sense if the bear represents too much, too big of any aspect of life. If it is this latter, I want to think about what in my life is too much and too big and what relationship do I really want with this "otherness," that which is "not me"; fear inducing; and, perhaps, not what it appears to be.

ROCKY: This thing is large. I move toward it. I can't do anything to it.

Rocky does not live in the world of subject and object nor does he reflect on experience. He is completely unified. Is he conscious? Does it matter? What is it that motivates him to chase or run toward some things? What moves him? Perhaps he has a connection to the apparent object that is unseen and tangible. He seems to have this connection. Loy (1999) said:

> If the Tao is nondual, it is not the 'I' that names and intends, but rather the reverse: subjectivity—the sense of a subjective consciousness that is doing the seeing, acting, and so on—arises because of the naming and intending. Without these activities—for example, in Taoist 'mindfasting'—the self evaporates." (p. 121)

Is Rocky mindfasting, or is he mindless? He is presumably less capable of mindfull activity than a person, and when in a state of instinctual response, probably whatever capacity he has to differentiate is diminished to zero. So, while Rocky may not be a true Daoist, perhaps, he can still be in touch with the Dao even though he is unconscious about this. Of course, Rocky may only look like a dog!

> BEAR: What do these small beings know of what is real? I can help them to learn.
> The bear has transcendent, god-like qualities. He seems to "look down upon."
> ROCKY: I must run toward this large being.
> LITTLE AVI: If I run away, I will never face the fear of that which seems overwhelming, and I will be separated from that which I love, Rocky (instinct), and that to which I need connection to G_d!?

IDENTITIES TRANSFORMING

> LITTLE AVI: I am aware that a bear is coming. Here he is. He is enormous. I must get away. Rocky is in danger. He never listens when I call him when something attracts his attention. He could be killed. I do not want to lose him and I do not want to be killed myself. I am struggling to get up the stairs, which are very steep. Rocky is running toward the bear. The bear seems unconcerned. Rocky is barking and darting toward the bear. The bear is looking off into the distance. He is very large.

ROCKY: Wow! Look at this bear. I have to meet with him. I will greet him by barking. I love running around and barking. I love this bear. He is not even looking at me. I can run at him and bark, and it is just so great. I am very happy.

BEAR: I am! I am! I am! I am moving! I love this little dog. He is full of joy. Look at little Avi running away. He doesn't know that he needs to come and meet me. I am the dream unfolding that he has and will become. He will know the meaning of this when he comes down the stairs and moves toward me. He needs to join with me and Rocky, but he is too afraid just now.

SPACE: I am in between Avi, the bear, and Rocky. I am empty, waiting to be filled. I am potential. I am light. I can be filled with anything. These three can move to any locations within me. They can realize their potential freedom to choose where they will be. They can be anywhere within me and in any relationship to each other.

LITTLE AVI'S HOUSE: I am safety and security. What is all that noise? What is wrong? Oh, oh, a bear! Rocky!? Avi, what are you doing? Be careful! WHAT ARE YOU DOING? Someone could be hurt or killed. Why isn't anyone listening to me? I cannot move. Avi and Rocky are only safe within me.

This house sounds like my mother—my Jewish mother—who was committed to trying to protect and control in the service of safety and security. She conveyed her worry and fear through words and tone.

THE STAIRS: I am very steep. I am making it difficult for Avi to get away from the world and into the wombness of house. He needs to face the world, but his house beckons, calls, and warns. The house is very seductive. I am the transition between outer and inner. I think Avi has spent so much time inside and he needs to balance by being more outside. I can only do so much. The pull of the house is very strong.

These stairs sound a lot like my father. He ushered me into the world. However, his influence was much less than my mother. He was away too much, and he was often emotionally away even when he was physically present.

THE FOREST: I am dark and mysterious. There are many things within me. To know me and what is in me, you must enter into my depths. Sometimes, I will allow something to emerge into the light, like the bear, but what emerges may be something disguised as something else. It will be in the form it is for a reason. The process of penetrating the form is as essential as is finding what is at its core.

THE SKY: I am above. Even as a child Avi felt that he would be safer if he was in me, above things, looking down on that which scared him from a safe place. It seemed less dangerous to him up here. I remember how as a child in his waking state, he decided that he would learn to fly in his dreams in order to escape from the danger of monsters and dangerous people that populated his dreams at times. He was successful at learning to fly in his dreams.

THE GROUND: Avi is afraid to be on me, grounded. Being grounded represents danger, suffocation, and lack of opportunity. He needs to be much more at home with me.

Identification with the parts, development of relationships between them, and use of awareness brings me an enhanced sense of wholeness, aliveness, and integration. I have become the parts, and they have become me.

DREAMING ON...

The dream continues. I will imagine what comes next. There is only one rule—to dream whatever is within the realm of my dreaming capacity.

ER: What's that about? What are you talking about?

AVRAHAM: Most dreams are representations of unfinished situations, unfinished personal situations. The unfolding possibility exists in the unconscious. Dreaming on is a way to access the unconscious process that has been unable to emerge. I assume that whatever a person can imagine comes from their unconscious and is representative of what is trying to happen. Bringing this to the surface of consciousness is a transformation of possibility into a vision, a map. From there the dreamer can begin to turn dreaming into being in the world.

LITTLE AVI: I am struggling to get up the stairs. I realize that Bear is not chasing me and is not attacking or harming Rocky. I pause. My heart is pounding. I suddenly think, "This is an inner emergency. Nothing actually merits my response." Now I have a competing thought. "Bears are dangerous. They kill small dogs and eat people."

I realize my response is not without basis, but I can't ignore that this bear has not done anything dangerous so far or in the moment. I have a problem. What is real? What does this bear want? Why isn't he behaving as I believe bears do? He seems to be looking off somewhere— somewhere very far away. What to do? I want my dog to be safe. My heart is pulled to Rocky who now comes complete with the bear. I don't want to falsely accuse the bear but he is very large and powerful and his species is known to be potentially dangerous. I have a very ambivalent attitude to that which is surely "not me." Should I respond to what I perceive, what I have actually witnessed, or should I respond to what is most often reported about bears? Should I entertain the possibility of entering this experience as if I have no preconceptions and no prior knowledge? I have stopped my struggle, my movement in the world. I am becoming conscious of other possibilities. The external movement has shifted to internal movement and creation of potential. At this point, is it, as Jacques Daignault (2002, lecture, University of British Columbia, Faculty of Education, Vancouver, Canada) describes, an actual reality that has emerged from the virtual?

BEAR: I love that I can see forever. I have to appear in a form. I have chosen the form of a bear. I am Bear and not Bear. I appear as Bear, but I am something else. If I were to appear in my true form, the little dog would still respond instinctually. Avi would be overwhelmed by the light. I am light, but I appear as form, animal form. I am in a perpetual process of becoming. I am never complete. I am always moving toward a horizon that is eternally moving away.

ROCKY: This is fun! This bear is fantastic. I am running and barking. I feel free and wild. Where is little Avi? Oh good, he has stopped trying to escape up those steep stairs. Can he tell that what he sees and what is are not exactly the same? Maybe he can join the bear, recognize that the space between us is an illusion, and that the space both separates and joins us. It is not one or the other. I am excited!

Rocky has transformed. He is now becoming conscious and self-reflective.

THE SYMBOLS IN THE DREAM

BEAR: A friend who is awkward that will help you if you are kind to him or her. Can also represent basic instincts, motherly protectiveness, strength, entering a new stage of life. Can also represent "fears," as a bear is a big scary thing for most of us.

DOG: Represents the dreamer's instincts, manliness.

CHASE: The dreamer fears physical attack; can mean the dreamer is avoiding dealing with difficult issues, especially if recurring in a nightmare form.[14]

A "rule" of dream interpretation is to never rely on standardized interpretations of dream symbols. Yet there does seem to be some truth in these descriptions for me.

PROCESS DESCRIPTION

What follows is intended to be as "bare bones" as possible. It is an attempt to describe without interpretation so that the dream experience stands on its own as itself and the process sequence and pattern are exposed.

1. I am in my front yard, which is not a yard with which I am actually familiar. *I am in a familiar location that I do not know.*
2. My dog, Rocky, a Bedlington Terrier, is there. *A small animal that I have a connection to is there.*

3. I become aware that a bear is approaching. *I know intuitively that something large and dangerous is coming.*
4. I cannot see the bear. *The danger is not visible.*
5. He is coming from some woods. *The danger is coming from an area into which I cannot see.*
6. I "know" he is coming. *My intuition of the presence of something is accurate.*
7. I am frightened. *The unknown is accompanied by fear.*
8. I call Rocky. *I call to the small being with whom I am connected.*
9. I am very frightened. *Fear is within me.*
10. I am afraid for him and for myself, and I am afraid of losing him. *Fear persists and includes the fear of loss and even death.*
11. I am scrambling up the extraordinarily steep stairs. I am having trouble getting up the stairs. *I struggle to get up and away. The struggle is difficult and increasingly challenging.*
12. Rocky is doing what he often does. He is ignoring me. I am having great difficulty ascending the stairs, and I am very frightened that the bear will kill him. *That which matters is in danger, and I have no influence.*
13. The bear appears. He is a gigantic, blue, black Kodiak bear; at least 10 feet tall. Rocky is small and has no sense of the danger and no fear. He rushes up to the bear, barking and making darting movements toward the bear. *There is a juxtaposition between the bear and Rocky. They have something in common—no fear and the ground.*
14. The bear is looking off to some far distant place. He pays no attention to Rocky. *The bear is visionary. Rocky is excited and focused.*
15. I continue to call Rocky and struggle to climb the stairs to the safety of the house and the front door to which I long to be on the other side. *Continuing to call and struggle for perceived safety does not succeed.*

ESSENCE OF THE DREAM

As Bear, I am stillness. As Rocky, I am ecstasy. As me, I am fear and love. Bear is like the eternal Dao that has always been and will always be. I am all things, everywhere, transcendent and whole. As Rocky, I am Azeem, the Dervish, the great one, the ecstatic. As me, I am fear and love. As fear, I am composed of opposing forces of energy and oppression. I want to express and be looked after, and I am afraid and holding back. I am love, drawn toward potential destruction. Does love create destruction, or does destruction create love?

Can the four of us come together? I wonder—can a bear, a dog, a scared little kid, and me live happily ever after?

THREE LEVELS OF MEANING FOR MY DREAM

1. *Personal.* Part of me is flesh and blood. Part of me is spiritual. I identify this part as a very large Kodiak bear. It is "not me." I look at spirit and see Bear. My inability to see through to reality is generating fear. Freedom is truly to do and be what I am meant to be. When I am free, I have no fear, or at least, it is not debilitating. I have and do not have the consciousness. Another part of me is ecstatic, instinctual, and free. This is embodied in my dog. Part of me is very afraid of that which I feel could injure or kill me. I identify most strongly with this part. This fits with my personal history. I was always told, "Be careful," "Don't run around. You'll get sweated up and get sick," and "Why would you want to do that" in reference to anything that was seen as difficult or risky. My unconscious is striving to identify these three parts and is demonstrating their simultaneous separation and integration. Perhaps, I can own my aggression, my instinct, and my spirit.

   I am reminded of the story of Hildegarde von Bingen who was a nun in the 13th century. She was talented and well loved. She was cloistered, shy, introverted, and subject to a patriarchal church, which did not create any dissonance for her. She did have a problem, however. She was quite ill. She wrote to Saint Bernard, who passed the message on to Pope Eugenuis, who surprisingly encouraged her in her work. She was reluctant but began to allow her talents more freedom of expression. She spent more time with people and was renowned for her healing powers and produced art and music. The more expressive she became, the healthier she was. Eventually, she lived into her 80s, which was very unusual at that time.

This story speaks to the importance of authenticity and listening and following one's true calling as a path to wholeness, transcendence, and health.

2. *World*. The world is full of fear. The spiritual is seen as large, scary, and removed from human experience; maybe it is not real. Only the instinct runs toward it, but humans eschew instinct. Freud's influence, which was an outgrowth of the Victorian culture within which he lived, was that instinct untamed and uncontrolled was dangerous. Man required a strong ego and super-ego to contain this potential.

3. *Spiritual*. The spiritual dimension and humans seem to often be "separated." It seems to be surprisingly unresponsive to the instinctual drive to connect with it, or alternatively, it is just there for me anytime I come and in any way. The Dao-field just is. Humans are either in touch with it or not.

MISSING ELEMENTS IN MY DREAM

There is often an emphasis on what has happened to people that has caused them harm. I take the position that what has happened is more importantly seen as a representation of what is or was missing. For example, if a person is abused as a child, this is, of course, a terrible experience; however, I believe this is distracting from the real issue, which is the love, care, and attention that was not there for that child. Spotting what is missing is not easy; the process of seeking is valuable, and the location of what is missing and naming of represents a big step in the transformation of psychological damage into psychological gold—alchemical healing.

The three living things in my dream are in a relationship and are not obviously relational. I am running away. Rocky is hurling himself toward the bear. The bear is looking off into the distance. There seems to be a connection, but there is no obviously relational behavior. The closest is Rocky, and he is drawn by instinct.

What is missing? Warm engagement. I need to move toward the bear and Rocky. The relationship needs to transform. I need encouragement, a guide, a helping hand, and a sense of security and safety. I remember a family friend who was my not-aunt, Auntie Evelyn. I always felt well received and accepted by her.

Auntie Evelyn is now present in my dream field. She represents protection and encouragement. "Come!" she says. "You will be safe with me." I feel my need for accompaniment. I feel different. I will go to the bear and Rocky. I put my hand in hers. She and I walk toward the bear and Rocky. When I am with her, I can do anything. I come to the bear. He is large and beautiful. I touch his coat. He looks down. I know that I am safe. Rocky calms down. The four of us are like one. There is the spirit bear, the instinct dog, the innocent boy, and the force of the maternal protector. Together, we form a quaternity.

> **Quaternity** \Qua*ter"ni*ty\, n. [LL. quaternitas, fr. L. quaterni four each: cf. F. quaternit['e].]
> 2. The union of four in one, as of four persons;—analogous to the theological term trinity. (Webster, 1913)

UNCERTAINTY

Stephen Mitchell (2002) gives a very succinct description of the "uncertainty principle" as defined by the physicist, Werner Heisenberg:

> ...One cannot ascertain and describe both the velocity and the position of an electron at the same time. To determine its velocity

is to change its position. To determine the position is to alter its velocity. Learning about something in the external world requires interacting with it, and that interaction has an impact on, changes, the thing one is studying. (p. 109)

This has implications for the understanding of my dream. Attending to the dream and aspects of life is an instance of life being observed, and the very fact of the observing changes that which is observed. As well, in the act of naming it (the dream), it changes. From the perspective of the dream each component has in our method an ability to observe aspects of the dream and so to see it and also to alter it through such observation.

Uncertainty is demonstrated by little Avi. The bear seems to be on a path. Rocky is going for the bear with no deviation. I am frightened. If I am in motion, I am not reflective, and if I am reflective, I am not moving. Perhaps, a more whole me can move and be reflective simultaneously.

Culturally and personally, I am predisposed to look for clarity and certainty, to search for solutions, and to look for closure. The alternative is not knowing, opening up, and looking more deeply into things and into the living inquiry[15] process, that is, being reflective. If there is to be any understanding, it is more likely to emerge through the process of inquiry. The depth, breadth, and meaning may become more obvious even as the possibility of a solution or an answer becomes less.

PRIMARY AND SECONDARY PROCESS

Amy Mindell (2002) suggests an exercise to create a dream based on the process structure of an individual. She says "that our ability to create a dream depend[s] largely on our capacity to transpose the [person's] process structure into symbolic images and place these elements together in a dream or story sequence" (p. 180). My primary process structure can be described as very intuitive and involved, and my secondary process, the part with which I do not identify, is running away from trouble, getting above it, or looking for a place of security from which I can make sense of things. This is what I extract from my dream and what I see as true about me. The gold lies within the secondary process.

I will only begin to have choice when I can take ownership of my secondary process, the part of my experience with which I do not identify. Let me try and do this:

"I am a person who, when frightened, wants to get away from what is frightening to me." I can say and write these words, but do I feel ownership of them? Not really. How about if I take a step back and talk about myself from a separate position. "You are a person who, when he is frightened, wants to get away from what is frightening and then move away with justifying thoughts." That feels more like it. I can talk about myself as another who is fearful. I don't seem to be able to make the shift to be that person who is frightened and owns it. How about if I own my unwillingness? "I am a person who doesn't want others to see that I am afraid." That feels real to me and is a bit surprising. I am also aware that I don't want to leave this last part in print for you, the reader, to see. I hadn't quite realized that. So, I am a person who is often afraid. When I am afraid, I want to cover this up and move away so no one will see and so I can feel less fearful and avoid feeling any embarrassment.

There are two things emerging; my fear of being seen when I am vulnerable and my consciousness when I am fearful. The latter must come first. With consciousness, I have the possibility of choice to not be run by my feelings. Amy Mindell (2002) goes on to describe how "the dream reveals a flow over time and, simultaneously, the entire dream is happening in any given moment" (p. 181). I would describe myself as intuitive—I know the bear is coming before he appears—quirky, making moves or statements that are idiosyncratic, not under conscious control, and often trying to find the "safer" place. These are actions that I take at times and for which I often have a "good" explanation.

Let us move on and find out what the dream community has to say about this dreaming.

THE DREAM COMMUNITY

The dream community is comprised of people who hear my dream, share their responses, and who then have my dream in their collective consciousness. These people also seem to be awakening within the dreaming experience.

July 20, 2002: I am at the Second Annual International Conference on Personal Meaning. I have an idea and decide to act on it. I make a direct request to meet with one of the keynote speakers, Dr. Ernesto Spinelli (2002, personal communication), Professor of Psychotherapy, Counselling and Counselling Psychology, and Academic Dean of the School of Psychotherapy and Counselling at Regent's College, London. Dr. Spinelli is one of the top existential analysts in the world and a multipublished author. He enthusiastically agrees to meet with me. In our meeting, he describes how he works with dreams and characterizes this as representative of work in däsanalysis, existential therapy. He tells me that from the existential perspective, a dream is taken as real—not that it takes place in the world but that it is a real event in consciousness, and the starting point is acceptance of the dream in content and process as it is. He goes on to say that dreams are statements, not ways out. They are ways of expressing a way of being. He says that the dream can be broken down into world components, characters, environment, and action. He offers some questions in relation to dreams—how does "I" in the dream engage with elements of the dream, how do the elements of the dream relate to the dreamer and to each other, what is the mood of the world? He summarizes his comments, "Something occurs in the interaction and relationship."

He reads the description of my dream and asks me some questions and then asks me to be Rocky being me. Temporarily, this suggestion paralyzes me. I can identify with Rocky, but somehow the request to be Rocky, the instinctual, confounds me. I am confused. Slowly, I realize that this is the problem. My instinct is encased within my identity, my identity that has been bestowed by my mother by her presence and by my father in his absence. It is an identity that is cautious and fearful. As Rocky, I want to follow my instinct, but I cannot move because of the outer shell that is not me. From an existential therapy perspective, this is just how it is. It is not necessary to do anything, but now I am confronted with choice. I have the option to change how I am in the world. This is both liberating and angst creating. I can no longer stay as I am without guilt for not living out my potential, and it does highlight my responsibility to make meaning and continually explore the questions that life poses.

July 21, 2002: I have a conversation with Dr. Arnold Mindell (2002, personal communication), the founder of Process-Oriented Psychotherapy. Arnold Mindell is a much-published author and an innovative and stimulating thinker. I tell him the dream. He suggests that the bear and Rocky are parts of me that I disown when I am in a state of fear. He suggests that the bear is G_d and that Rocky is the free, instinctual part of me. In particular, he suggests that the bear appears dangerous, as do my "critics," who "show up" most noticeably when I am in a situation that will elicit my performance anxiety. He "reminds" me that the bear is G_d and that my connection with the truth of the bear and Rocky is a connection with my authenticity and my spiritual nature. I feel inspired.

Arnold Mindell's suggestions are like the other side of the coin from the insights that came from my discussions with Dr. Spinelli. Arnold Mindell has identified that which is me, potentially, and that with which I am not identified, at least not when I am under duress. I am more aware of my edge, my personal identity limit, and my secondary process.

After this contact, I phone a friend and invite her for coffee. She cannot make it. I start out on my own with this essay in hand headed for a local café. I have a feeling to go elsewhere. I set out for Granville Island Marketplace. I arrive, buy coffee, and look for a table where I can write, observe the passing scene, and do more writing. I notice a large table and head toward it. One man sits there by himself. As I am sitting down, a young man who looks unhappy is cleaning up. The older man directs a comment to him about the day coming to an end soon. The young man seems not to notice.

The man (Morrison, 2002, personal communication) begins to speak to me. He is a middle-aged man with a welcoming face. His manner of speaking suggests to me that he is of First Nations background. He notes all my materials and asks, "Are you a writer or a scribbler?" I boldly state, "A writer." He tells me that he is writing a movie script, that he consults on films, is a lawyer, Haida, Cherokee, Scottish, and with a little bit of Jewish thrown in for good measure.

He tells me many things that are reminiscent of Carlos Castaneda's stories of the Yaqui Indian medicine man, Don Juan Mateus. His way of speaking suggests to me that he speaks from experience. He says, "A Haida warrior faces things alone with no thought that anyone will help. If someone helps, that's gravy." He also tells me, "Keep fear behind you. Don't let it get ahead of you. If you do that's trouble. Stop thinking." He goes on, "If I can still see it, it's after humans arrived on earth. If I can't see it, it's prior to humans being on earth."

I share my dream with him. He says, "Dreams can be reliving something that happened. They can also be information about how to deal with a situation that is not part of your normal experience."

He tells me that in the Haida language, there is no present tense. Everything is future perfect—in other words, in a continuous process of becoming. He gives an example, "If I say I am a man, I am finished, and if I say I am becoming a man, then the process is unfolding." This latter statement seems to me to be a liberation from the seemingly impossible task of being conscious in the dot of the present. The unfolding process of becoming seems so much more graspable and available to my consciousness—a meaningful revelation!

Finally, he says about my dream, "It seems like you're trying to get somewhere you're not supposed to be."

We talk for 2 hours. At the end of the time, he says something about taking up my time. I respond, "This is what my time was for this afternoon." He tells me that a gift can only be given properly if the recipient is worthy. He says this in a way that it seems that he has given a gift and that I have given him the gift of my worthiness. He departs at a brisk pace, limping slightly, an apparent vestige of the stroke that he told me he had a year ago. The crowd parts, and he disappears into the sea of late Sunday afternoon shoppers.

July 25, 2002: I have lunch with my friend and colleague, Larry Green (2002, personal communication), a psychotherapist. I tell him about my dream community and that I want him to be part of it. He agrees to join. I show him the dream and start to tell him what some others have said. He stops me, saying, "I don't want to be polluted by the other ideas."

He says, "Rocky represents the innocent, naïve part of you that ignores practical, world-wise advice. The bear can see something that you can't see. He knows what's really important."

That night I ask my friend, Camellia Rumball (2002, personal communication), to be part of my dreaming community. She says, "I am going to have a dream in relation to your dream. When I do, I will share the dream with you."

Two days later, she reported that she had had a dream as follows but could see no relationship and would try again:

> I am on stage teaching a yoga class. The audience wants me to bring my friend May, who is also a yoga teacher, up to instruct as well. I smile and agree, but internally I am not happy about this but do not show my displeasure; and I continue with the class, acting as if everything is fine, but it is not, and I am not.

When she tells me the dream, I see no obvious connection to my dream, which is unusual for me. I can usually see a connection between almost anything and everything. The next morning I awake, and while sitting in meditation. I am remembering that Camellia had a dream that did not relate to my dream. I cannot remember her dream. Suddenly her dream comes back. I put myself into the dream. Since it is in my consciousness, in a very real sense, it is now my dream. In particular, I am focused on the moments of peak feeling as described by Mahrer (1989) "when you actually have the experiencing, when bodily sensations come alive" (p. 191) and the sentient experiences as described by Arnold Mindell (2001):

> Ask yourself about your sentient experiences while in the neighbourhood of the dreamer. What is your deepest sense of being

while you're with this other person? Unspoken feelings you are having when you are near the dreamer give you a sense of his or her non-local Dreaming. Do you feel dizzy, happy, sad, tired, hemmed in, or...?

Sentient experience is non-local; that is, it knows no spatial boundaries. Therefore, you can explore how such experiences apply to both you and the other person. Sentient experience connects you to the other. Pay attention to your own or to the sentient experiences whenever possible. (p. 86)

So in my dream, I am on stage. I am teaching. The audience wants me to bring some one I know up to instruct as well. I smile and agree. Inside I am very upset and angry. I can feel this in my body. I do not have any thoughts that explain the feelings and their strength. I am acting as if everything is fine. I am a good actor.

I have put myself in Camellia's position and have the dream. I suddenly know with complete certainty that her dream is totally connected to my dream. In this iteration, the bear is my mother, and Rocky is my younger brother, Stephen, who was born when I was 4. He is instinctual and heads unerringly for mother bear. I am frightened by the threat. I love him and fear his instinctual nature and his needs. I call him to come as I am trying to move away from him and my now-threatening mother and toward security. I cannot get there. I am caught in an impossible dilemma. The house which is unreachable is also my mother. At four I have nowhere to go and no one to turn to.

Camellia has requested a dream that relates. She has received this dream and sees no relationship. Initially, I do not either. Now I do!

The dream is about my aloneness with which I am not able to cope at 4. I have been the one and only. In Camellia's dream, she is the one and only. We are both delivered competition. I am at a loss. At 4, I am too young. A half year later, we moved from Toronto to Vancouver. I lost my special friend who lived across the street. I was separated from my grandparents and all my aunts, uncles, and cousins. It is a poignant time, and I have no words, and my parent's ears are not sufficient either.

Life's exigencies are apparent at too early a point in my life. My choices are to give up or to struggle for meaning. At 4, an inward quest is catalyzed by life that continues to this day.

Camellia did not want to share the stage nor did I. I did not have the required inner resources. I needed support that was not available. She had to acquiesce in her dream to the demands and requirements of the environment and community as did I. She acts graciously and hides her anger. At 4, I did not act graciously, and I did not hide my upset and anger, although I could not articulate what it was about. These feelings continued for many years, and apparently the vestiges may still lurk in the dark recesses of my consciousness. I cannot GO HOME!

The theme I see in Camellia's dream is loss of primacy. I then see the same pattern in my dream in a more symbolic form. Her request provides a dream that reveals my dream as a major pattern from my personal history.

My little brother, represented by Rocky, is drawn to my mother represented by the bear. I am struggling to get to my mother, the house. The stairs, which represent transition, are very steep and hard to ascend, and I am not able to climb them to get to what I believe will be security. I cannot realize that there is no one home. My mother is not there anymore. She has given birth and been reborn as a new mother. My difficulty is terrifying and protective. I do not have the capacity to recognize and cope with my essential aloneness and that I have now been hurled into the world, alone. I am at the beginning of my existential dilemma in life. Camellia is also a first born and, like me, was the only child for 4 years. At 4, I am confronted with the beginning experience of a life-long question: Am I able to take responsibility for my life?

August 2, 2002: I am having coffee at Seattle's Best and working on this essay. One of the employees, Jim (2002, personal communication), the assistant manager, introduces himself and asks what I am doing. I tell him and ask if he wants to know the dream. He indicates he does. He reads it and says, "It's a test." This fits for me. It is a test of my identity and what I value. There is a pull for survival and toward an apparent higher calling. Jim goes back to work and then comes back a little later. He wants to know what the dream means. I tell him about edges and being caught between. He says, "That's me. I'm always in the middle. I want to change." I suggest that he can delve more deeply into his middle position. I also suggest that he can move more into the position of stepping back to get a better overview and see what might emerge. I talk about the Dao and when a person is stuck out of the Dao. He likes this. He tells me that he and his girlfriend are trying to make a decision about splitting up or staying together. The dream community is "at work."

August 3, 2002: Steve Schklar (2002, personal communication), an analytic psychotherapist, is visiting from Toronto. He agrees to be part of my community and starts by suggesting that the bear is mother and that she is disassociated, showing no interest in the children. In the light of day, when I am conscious, there is no security and no place to go. It seems that the mother bear is not concerned if the cubs are in sight. She is focused on the far off. Nurturing is missing. There is no emotional contact. He wonders if I want to go into the house to move into what is not conscious. He suggests that the external territory doesn't make sense and is scary.

He asks what happened at age 12. The first thought that comes to me is that I was preparing for my Bar Mitzvah and that I had a lot of anxiety about this. For me, it was the performance aspect, not the ritual passage into manhood, that it was supposed to represent.

He suggests that the dog represents a pre-oedipal state. There is no language and no separation between me as Rocky and the bear. This is the symbiotic state between mother and child. He says that the three living things represent parts of me that are not integrated, stages of my development, and the dream depicts the struggle for integration.

August 5, 2002: I meet with my friend, Alison Beaumont (2002, personal communication). She is a social worker with a Jungian and process-oriented background and she is also a writer. She has many years of experience working with dreams.

She posits that part of me wants contact with the bear and that the animals represent instincts. She notes that in my description I refer to the bear as "he." She also asks about what happened at age 12. She notes my Bar Mitzvah as a transition into adulthood and/or to my spiritual self.

She asks, "What are bears to you?" I respond, "Powerful, big, animal, scary, interesting."

She says that I seem more frightened for Rocky than for myself and that it is difficult for me to get to safety, which requires movement upward. She sees that I am doing things at this time, namely, a PhD, that will "move you up in the world," "take you to another realm," "move you up towards the spiritual."

She suggests that I am fearful for an unconscious part of me that is much loved and that is in danger from an unconscious and very powerful part of me that wants to be known. This latter comment reminds me of the statement of one of my original mentors, Dr. Peter Lavelle, who told me 30 years ago in no uncertain terms, "You are sitting on your power." Alison says, "You mustn't forget to love, and your dream seems to be about innocence!"

What has arisen for me next about the dream follows. I have another dream that is related.

> I am at the University of British Columbia with my very beautiful and appealing girlfriend. A friend, with whom I am not on good terms, is suddenly there. He starts to insinuate himself with her. I feel very uncomfortable and protective. Carl, my academic supervisor, is there. I introduce him to her.

I have over many years gotten in trouble by following my instinct and then withdrawing. The bear—here representing the feminine—has been unhappy with me. It is about how I follow instinct. As Rocky, I am unconscious. As me, I am unconscious. Either way, the bear becomes a thing and loses its individuality and humanness.

This is a remnant of my relationship with my grandmothers. I want to like them. I am drawn to them. I am repulsed by them. I am afraid of them and of being "drowned" or suffocated by them.

In the new dream, I am happy to be with my girlfriend. My friend from whom I am alienated is there. I feel threatened and helpless. Carl is there. I acknowledge him, and he meets my lover. Perhaps, I am introducing my feminine aspect to him.

As me, I am also instinctual. I am fear driven. I am the opposite of Rocky. He moves toward and feels excited. I move away and feel terrified. The bear is what it is and what it is not! Can the instinctual be conscious? I feel now that the bear needs protection from instinct. It will either attach or be left alone and lonely. I am also the bear who is attached or abandoned.

ANOTHER BEAR

If the bear is G_d, he is not the all-knowing, all-powerful G_d as described in the Judeo-Christian tradition but a G_d full of angst and despair and also containing a huge sense of vision and potential. If Rocky represents a part of me that is drawn unerringly to G_d, then little Avi represents a part of me that runs in fear from G_d and runs toward security and comfort behind a door rather than face the truth. Apparently, G_d is struggling in a similar though different way with His relationship to humanity.

The divine and the human long for connection. The divine seems to lack the knowledge as to how to manifest this union, make it known that the union is already there, or is capricious or mysterious in its implementation of the connection; the human has a crisis of courage related to the desire for this union. The conflict is played out on the earth, under the sky, in an open space between the forest of the unknown and the house of security, behind a door that would block contact and even vision.

This is both a human and divine dilemma, and as Buber (1979) says, "When we walk our way and encounter a man who comes toward us, walking his way, we know our way only and not his; for his comes to life for us only in the encounter" (p. 124). The human and the divine are struggling together to have the encounter and to avoid it. Both actions take place in the same moments.

As the bear, I have an incredible vision and love, and I often feel alone with it and lonely. As Rocky, I have no pause for reflection. I must be near the bear. If I pause, I will recognize his pain and that little Avi is afraid and going the other way. I know the joy of being with the bear.

As little Avi, I am full of fear. The divine is only dimly recognizable. I am fearful and alone, and I am alienated from the part of me that knows a relationship with G_d through Rocky, who is a Christ-like figure, and has no choice but to be with G_d.

I am the bear. I am Rocky. I am little Avi. I am an all too frail human being.

And what of my Aunt Evelyn? She is the missing maternal, feminine principle—the relational, joining element. She can be the "fourth," who brings the three together. She requires them to do her calling, and they require her to achieve union—the human and the instincts, the human, the instinct, and the divine. The divine also needs the union with the human and the instinct to achieve wholeness.

DEEPER INTO THE BEAR

Thursday, August 7, 2002: I awake feeling anxious and lonely, in a dark place within myself. I decide to look for the personal meaning buried within this experience. I am aware that I feel a lack of connection to people at the moment I am writing this. I realize that many people see me like the bear. At times, I feel like the bear. When I am the bear who moves and sees in the world in powerful ways, I feel strong and independent. At other times as the bear, I recognize my own isolation and otherness. A memory emerges. As a very young child, I recognized that being smart had a cost. Other children referred to eggheads. Some just drew back. I knew that my mental agility had the potential to cause me to be rejected and alienated.

> BEAR: I am powerful. I see far. I have moments of great connection, and I am often alone and not always easy with this. I am forever an outsider.

I have always been the bear with the little kid and the dog inside me. I remember my teacher and Gestalt therapist, David Berg. David was a philosophy professor at Simon Fraser University in Burnaby, British Columbia. He trained as a Gestalt therapist with Fritz Perls at Lake Cowichan, British Columbia. He had a huge intelligence and he was a very large man physically. I always remember thinking, "No one could get their arms around him". He was married and had children. He got caught somewhere between the bear, the kid, and the dog. He took his own life. I was devastated. If David couldn't get out of the bear trap, then what was the meaning of all that work I had done with him? I began to realize that question may be the way in. I have continued to search for the elusive grail. Searching seems to be an answer of some sort. What else is there to do?

Part of my problem is what was suggested by my experience with Dr. Spinelli. I have trouble as a result of the instinctual side of me being contained within my persona. The personality that I present to the world is in conflict with my inner experiences. What I mean by this is the problem that is familiar to most people, the problem of incongruence; appearing one way and being another. This is not a problem that is as simple as mere dishonesty, which it is at some level. It is about the core conflict in me between being and representing who I truly am.

How to Have a Happy Ending

I thought that the previous paragraph was the end of this essay and then I thought, "What a downer! No one will want to read this." So now you, my dear reader, are incorporated ever more deeply into my thoughts and feelings about all this. I am now dreaming about you, me, and our relationship and hoping that you will read this essay and find it meaningful. This is a moment of writing and "living" in a space of nonlocality and nontemporality as described by Arnold Mindell (2001):

> The Dreaming is similar... Furthermore, what you notice in this world, as it arises into Dreamland and everyday reality, greatly

depends on how open you are to the arising experiences and to your personal 'dictionary' of descriptions.

From the viewpoint of Dreaming, the ever-changing patterns attributable to the interactions between Dreaming and everyday life are awesome: the perpetually changing awesomeness is the point. (pp. 152–153)

If you experience the altered states of consciousness connected to the Dreaming, however, images become less significant than the sense of eternal change and the energy of impermanence...

I try to understand the significance of memory loss. It often seems that when the Big You is not interested in something, your memory begins to give you trouble. (p. 155)

Bear is the big me who doesn't remember feeling lonely. Then I have trouble. If I want to live well, I have to acknowledge that I am, at times, living as the persona that is represented by the bear and that is not who I am at certain moments. I am frozen into this role and the vulnerable me, little Avi, and the free me, Rocky, are captured inside. The little kid has been and continues to be an escape artist, a frequent fleer, and Rocky has always been magnetized to whatever attracted him.

I remember a time when I was quite young, about 8. I was an excellent reader and was chosen to participate in radio shows at the CBC for school children. I took great delight in this and had no fear, only joy, at the performance opportunity. I remember on one occasion feeling I had done something particularly well, and subsequently, I almost missed a cue, but I didn't. I was about a half a beat slow. That was the last show I recall doing. I don't know if my memory is accurate, but there is an internal connection. Mess up, lose out.

In grade 12, I was reading aloud in Mr. Hunter's English class. I noticed I was very shaky and having trouble speaking. I had no idea what was happening. I subsequently became increasingly avoidant about public speaking opportunities.

Recently, I can feel the little boy, who longing to run free, is like the little dog, having a resurgence, pushing to transcend the bear persona, integrate the bearness, move toward my destiny, my potential....

At this point, I will let my dream go into space, your space. If you have read this far, you now know my dream pretty well. You are a part of my dreaming community. Since you know the dream in your own consciousness, in a very real sense, it is now your dream. Perhaps, you would like to dream this dream in the ways suggested by the exercise and see what experience emerges, or you may have some other way of having the dream and the dreaming, or maybe just use it with your own dream. Don't hesitate to invite me into your dreaming community.

So, what is the true meaning of this dream? As you see, I have imputed different meanings at different times. In the spiritual domain, there are suggestions and experiences about altered states, the dreaming process, and G_d. All has substance and meaning for me at the moment. In particular, the inherent contradictions are meaningful for me.

> That bear is slow moving. That dog is fast moving. That boy is trying to get away.
> I am slow moving. I am fast moving. I am trying to get away.
> I am the bear. I am the dog. I am that boy.
> I am forest. I am sky. I am ground. I am stairs. I am home.
> I am calm. I am excited. I am afraid.
> I am more empty space than solid mass.

I AM that which is all these things. I am that which knows. I am the story teller and the story. I am the sum of all things that converge at this point and who is becoming that which is still being created.

I AM NEW... POSTSCRIPT(S)

I had another dream a month ago.

> I am in my office. I open the door. It opens directly onto the hallway—unlike my actual office, which opens to the waiting room. I see an estranged male friend and a woman whom I know well, hugging. He is apparently on his way to the doctor next door. I know this woman to be very vivacious and someone who loves to learn by experience. I am surprised. They separate, and he continues down the hall. I say rather lamely and in an attempt to be ironic, "They'll let anyone in here."

This dream seems to be a different form of my dogbearAvi dream. I am observing. I am shaken. My former friend is like Bear. He is a threat to me. My client is like Rocky. Running toward whatever attracts her attention in order to find out what 'it' is.

I realize that I am often in the observer role, and the role of Rocky, the bold adventurer, is often disowned. I used this observation in a circumstance where I was scheduled to speak in front of a large number of people. I recognize that the audience is Bear. In my state of fear, I am little Avi. I become Rocky, and I cannot wait to be with Bear. In the actual event prior to speaking, I am little Avi. As soon as I stand up, I am Rocky and I want to engage with Bear. It goes very well. I feel calm.

June 28, 2003: I meet with my friend, Hamid. He has read an earlier version of this essay. He suggests that when I am struggling to get up the stairs, I am climbing Jacob's ladder and that perhaps there is something I need in the house. I feel an internal resistance to this idea. I don't want to go back. I realize that I must. There is something there that I still need, and without it, I cannot leave the inner world of the house behind and live fully in life.

...and the pluperfect name he gave it: Jacob's Ladder.

The name comes from a story in the Old Testament book of Genesis, about a dream that young Jacob had:

> "... And behold a ladder set up on the earth, and the top of it reached to heaven: and behold the angels of God ascending and descending on it. And behold, the Lord stood above it, and said, I am the Lord...I am with thee, and will keep thee in all places whither thou goest, and will bring thee again into this land...." (28: 12–15, King James version).

> ....There's a subsequent story (Genesis 32:24–30) of what may have been part of Jacob's struggle for self-definition: "And Jacob was left alone; and there wrestled a man with him until the breaking of day..." The outcome: "I have seen God face to face, and my life is preserved."

ILLUSTRATION **2.** *Jacob's Ladder,* 1800–1803.

Watercolor by William Blake, 1757–1827 (Blake, 1800–1803).
Reproduced by permission from Art Ticknor of the SelfDiscovery Portal,
http://www.selfdiscoveryportal.com/index.htm.

Jacob is depicted as asleep and dreaming of a spiral staircase by which angels commune between man and God. The inclusion of humans on the ascending staircase emphasizes Blake's interpretation of this dream as a metaphor for the soul's aspiration to be reunited with God.

So, if I dream on, I am climbing the stairs and leaving the worldly experience behind. I reach the door. It opens by itself. I enter. It is like no home I have ever known, and it is home; it is the home of all homes. I feel a great sense of piece and security. There is a brilliant light that seems as if seeing would be impossible, and yet I can see, although I have no words for what I am seeing. I am seeing the essence, the essence of all things. Suddenly a fireball comes toward me. I am not afraid. I want to experience this fireball. It enters my chest. I am infused with a burning energy. I am whole, and in my wholeness, I am not any solid matter, only space. I am empty, and the emptiness has consciousness. I have to descend the ladder and return to life in the material world. I will return with what I have gained and share this with Bear, Rocky, forest, ground, sky, empty space, and you.

EVEN MORE...

There is seemingly no end to this writing and dreaming. Some experiences never go away. I talk to Arnold Mindell, tonight—July 27, 2003. I need to talk about the bear, Rocky, and little Avi again. It has become apparent to me that the fear within me is not easily put to rest. I relate my fears of Bear to my fears of body symptoms, which relate to my fears of the embodied Nazi; Bear represents a power to kill. I get a glimmer of how this power used consciously can work for me and others. As Avi, I am living out the message from my mother, "Be careful! If you get all worked up, you will get sick!" What a message to give an energetic, not-fearful kid. "Geez, Mum, give me a break. I need to live." I am dissociated from the Rocky in me. That's why he appears in my dream as an out of control dog. If I run wild, I could die. If I say what is true, it could be dangerous.

I remember in my family that there was a huge prohibition on talking about "unpleasant" things such as accidents, sickness, and death.

I guess that if it isn't talked about it, then it didn't exist—fertile ground for fear/full/ness.

I have a memory of being at the doctor's with my mum. I am about 4. He wants to look into my mouth. I am not favorably disposed to this. He holds me down on an examining table with his body weight and attempts to open my mouth. I respond. I dig my teeth into the fleshy part at the base of his thumb. He stops. I am relieved and frightened. What will be the consequence of my action? I learn another bad lesson. Defending myself against the attacking bear leads to anticipation, the anticipation of retaliation. I don't recall that anything actually happened, but I know I have always had fears about being very assertive.

Little Avi is like a natural child. When unsafe, he runs away to his mother. If I don't like what is happening, I can do this. I can also sniff it out like Bear, and I can dive in like Rocky.

The dreaming process is in my body. I need to pay attention to the dreaming. If I am afraid, I need to explore the fear, which means to feel it. There is wisdom in the dreaming of the body. The Jews have learned to be afraid of the body. It can do a lot of damage, and it can suffer. I am living out the fears of my cultural heritage. This is not an easy edge to transcend. My work is not just for me. It is for all the Jews, even the ones who are not Jewish.

THE NEVER-ENDING DREAM

You and I have a bear that is visionary and completely serene; a dog, Rocky, who is absolutely curious and has to know without any real concern for consequences; a little Avi who is young, terrified and conflicted, a sky that is overarching and above, a ground that is supportive and basic, an underground that is hidden, a forest that beckons, threatens, and contains treasures dark, bright, and unknown, and a spaciousness that in its emptiness is connective between all the various parts of you, me, and all things. My dream is now your dream and our dream. There are mysteries yet to be uncovered. I anticipate their discovery by us.

References

Blake, W. (1800–1803). *Jacob's ladder*. Retrieved on June 15, 2003, from http://www.selfdicoveryportal.com/arJacobsladder.htm

Buber, M. (1970). *I and thou*. New York: Charles Scribner and Sons.

Capra, F. (1988). *Uncommon wisdom: Conversations with remarkable people*. New York: Simon & Shuster Inc.

Cohen, A. (2002). The secret of effective psychotherapy: Metaskills. *The Private Practitioner Bulletin of the Canadian Counselling Association, 1*(3), 3.

Diamond, J., & Spark-Jones, L. (2004). *A path made by walking: Process work in practice*. Portland, OR: Lao Tse.

Gibran, K. (2001). *The prophet* . UK: Wordsworth.

Hahn, T. N. (1998). *The heart of the Buddha's teaching: Transforming suffering into peace, joy, and liberation*. New York: Broadway Books.

Jones, L. S. (in press). Feasting in possibility: Process work research in postmodern times. *Journal of Process Oriented Psychology*. Portland, OR: Lao Tse Press.

Jung, C. G. (1989). *Memories, dreams, and reflections* (R. Winston & C. Winston, Trans.). New York: Vintage.

Loy, D. (1999). *Nonduality: A study in comparative philosophy*. Amherst, New York: Humanity Books.

Mahrer, A. (1989). *Dream work in psychotherapy and self-change*. Markham, ON, Canada: Penguin.

Mindell, Amy. (2002). *Alternative to therapy*. Newport, OR: Zero Publication.

Mindell, Arnold. (2000). *Working with the dreaming body*. Portland, OR: Lao Tse Press. (Original work published 1984)

Mindell, Arnold. (1985). *River's way: The process science of the dreambody*. Boston: Routledge & Kegan Paul.

Mindell, Arnold. (2000). *Inner dreambody work: Working on yourself alone*. Portland, OR: Lao Tse Press. (Original work published 1990)

Mindell, Arnold. (2001). *The dreammaker's apprentice: Using heightened states of consciousness to interpret dreams*. Charlottesville, VA: Hampton Roads.

Mitchell, S. A. (2002). *Can love last: The fate of romance over time*. New York: W.W. Norton & Co.

Moustakas, C. (1988). *Phenomenology, science, and psychotherapy*. Cape Breton, NS, Canada: University College of Cape Breton, Family Life Institute.

Moustakas, C. (1990). *Heuristic research: Design, methodology, and applications*. Newbury Park, CA: Sage Publications.

Moustakas, C. (1994). *Existential psychotherapy and the interpretation of dreams*. Northvale, NJ: Jason Aronson.

Moustakas, C. (1995). *Being in, being for, being with*. Northvale, NJ: Jason Aronson.

Perls, F., Hefferline, R. F., & Goodman, P. (1951). *Gestalt therapy: Excitement and growth in the human personality*. New York: Dell Publishing.

Perls, F. S. (1947/1969). *Ego, hunger, and aggression: The gestalt therapy of sensory awakening through spontaneous personal encounter, fantasy, and contemplation*. Toronto, ON, Canada: Random House.

Tulku, T. (2000). Lucid dreaming: Exerting the creativity of the unconscious. In G. Watson, S. Batchelor & G. Claxton (Eds.), *The psychology of awakening: Buddhism, science, and our day-to-day lives* (pp. 271–283). York Beach, ME: Samuel Weiser.

Webster's Revised Unabridged Dictionary. (1913). Springfield, MA: Merriam Co.

CHAPTER 7

THE INNER PATH
AND OUTER EXPERIENCE
IN CLASSROOMS

Reflective practitioners conduct 'frame experiments' in which they impose a kind of coherence on 'messy' situations. They make sense of new and unusual situations by reframing them in light of past experience or previous knowledge. Reflective practitioners come to new understandings of situations through a spiraling process of framing, reframing, experimentations and 'back talk.' Thus, reflective practice goes beyond just being curious or intrigued about some aspect of one's practice (a commonly held conception) . . . . being curious or intrigued about one's practice is not equivalent to being reflective about one's practice. Reflective practitioners go beyond curiosity and intrigue to frame, reframe, and develop a plan for future action. Perhaps most importantly, it is the reframing stage that is critical, for it is at this stage that reflective practitioners construct new knowledge about their practice settings.

—Clarke (1994, pp. 498–499)

CONCERNS ABOUT THE CURRENT EDUCATIONAL PERSPECTIVE

Present-day education in Canada and the United States focuses on curriculum absorption and production and attends to human experience only when behavior is exhibited that interferes with absorption and production. This latter view casts humans as machine-like and needing to be fueled with ideas and motivation to produce. An example of this is the initiative by the government of British Columbia to increase funding for school-readiness programs for preschool children. The *Vancouver Sun* (Hansen, 2005) attributes the following to Shirley Bond, the minister of education for the government of British Columbia, "The government expanded the responsibilities of the Education Ministry to include concepts of learning and literacy for pre-school-age children, from newborn infants to six year olds" (p. 1). Surely we have to question the pressure this puts on children to perform cognitive tasks for which they may not be developmentally prepared in the service of ensuring their future job marketability. As well, we need to be deeply concerned about the time taken away from learning that is crucial to their development as vibrant human beings, who are alive with the wonder and joy of experiencing the world through their senses and emotions and who are becoming compassionate human beings capable of relating to others with love and care. More than anything, young children need to play, in both unstructured and structured ways, exploring their natural and social world in the company of each other and of adults who are loving and caring. Without doubt, the initiative to promote—at almost any cost—literacy and numeracy in preschool children is in line with efforts to move them into the system, through it, and out into the workforce as young adults at as rapid a rate as possible and, apparently, without any questions about the possible detrimental effects on vulnerable children who are our future leaders and citizens. Deborah Meier's (2005) comments in the *Harvard Education Newsletter* are relevant:

> We need to transform the world of childhood in school. American educators are almost always interested in moving children forward and upward faster, rather than allowing them to become

more deeply and broadly engaged in appropriate childhood tasks. An internally self-motivated child is often able to 'make up' for lost academic time. In Finland, children don't start to learn reading and writing until second grade but top the world in academic performance by the end of elementary school.

I am concerned about the direction for education that is supported by the Ministry of Education in British Columbia, which I believe is consistent with current directions in education in Canada. I believe that it is this achievement and production-oriented pedagogy that leads to a wounding experience in learners. This wounding takes the form of emotional blunting, and ignites the emergence of a variety of symptoms that inexorably leads to the surfacing of the "diagnostic industries"[16] and a complete de-emphasis of truly human experiences. The text quoted previously from the *Vancouver Sun* is the signal that this wounding is going to happen, and this is compounded by the embedded message that the early start of preparation for school is a good thing. An example from my own experience occurred when I was in grade 5. I was sitting in class and not attending to the lesson, as I was engaged in showing my baseball card collection to another little boy. I was especially proud of my collection as I had managed to accumulate some cards that were in very short supply and valuable even in those days. The teacher caught me and confiscated the cards. When I asked for them back after the class, he told me that he was going to throw them out and that there would be no discussion. I managed to speak with the school janitor, and asked if he would rescue the cards for me. He told me that he couldn't do that. I was extremely upset by this loss, but the message was clear. I was not there to have fun, at least not as I perceived fun. I was there to learn and anything that interfered with or deviated from the prescribed curriculum would be dealt with swiftly and severely. There was no interest in my feelings or needs. I became increasingly frightened of doing anything wrong in school, and this fear transferred to other areas of my life where there were authority figures. I learned that it was not a good idea to be excited about something, and increasingly, I became a child who did not exhibit exuberance and who did not tolerate it too well in others.

I learned that expressing my wants and needs was not going to have any positive effect, and I subsequently found this increasingly more difficult to do. This is my personal example of emotional wounding with subsequent blunting of emotional expression. I was not valued for being the curious and excited child that I was. I was punished for being that way and given the strongest possible message to stay focused on the person in charge and his or her instructions. While I believe that this wounding is serious enough in itself, perhaps even more serious is the loss of the drive to thrive and move toward the outer reaches of personal human possibilities. This is a personal experience. I believe that variations on this theme are played out over and over in the school system where children are given the message that who they are and what is personally important to them is not what is important. Children learn that what they can do is what will earn or not earn them love, belonging, and fulfillment in life.

This wounding starts from the earliest schooling experience and continues into adult education, which is where the reflections for this essay are based. I have seen these themes over and over in my practice as a humanistic psychotherapist and in my work as an educator. I am interested in the healing of these wounds in students and educators. I believe that my reflections and the reflections of my students stand in opposition to this dehumanizing and wounding direction and demonstrate the benefits of a human-centered approach to education.

PROCESS-ORIENTED, TRANSPERSONAL, AND HUMANISTIC PERSPECTIVES IN EDUCATION

I have wondered about possible alternatives to what seems to be an inhumane direction. I don't use this word *inhumane* lightly, but it seems to me that an education system that is mainly focused on production, achievement, and economic success and addresses the person most often when he or she stands out as falling through the cracks merits the word. This critique brings me to an approach to education that centralizes human beings and their experience in the classroom and that has curriculum learning as an important but secondary priority.

The transpersonal perspective states that a human being is more than an individual biophysical unit and has potential that transcends the individual and encompasses the experiential possibilities of the deeper mysteries of life. The transpersonal includes possibilities related to meditative practices, altered states, and ecstatic experiences. It acknowledges the spiritual and timeless dimension of experience. The idea that identity is larger than the personal and that there is a felt interblending of all things is opened up. Humanism emphasizes human potential and the inherent possibilities for learning and growth in human beings both individually and collectively. Transpersonal philosophy can be seen as related to humanistic philosophy. The transpersonal perspective acknowledges the human potential that transcends human experience. The suggestion is that an evolved human is capable of experiencing that which is numinous and beyond the rational and discursive realms. There is also the suggestion that the energy of the transpersonal realm can be "brought down" into the human dimension, subjectively and inter-subjectively. These philosophies are reflected in the real experiences described, as we shall see, by the students quoted in this essay.

Humanistic and transpersonal philosophies are not new. These approaches, the so-called Third Force, in the realm of psychotherapy began to emerge in the late 1950s as a reaction to the Second Force, that is, psychoanalysis, which was a reaction to the First Force of behaviorism. This Third Force placed an emphasis on personal responsibility, interpersonal and personal sensitivity, and the interblending and interconnectedness of all things from the apparently inert to the ineffable. In fact, transpersonal approaches are considered the Forth Force and encompass the idea that humans are more than flesh and blood and that the human potential includes knowledge and connection with the divine. While these approaches have not disappeared completely, neither have they ever become part of the mainstream. If it is such a good thing, why isn't there more respect paid to it than the present-day marginal positioning indicates? These paradigms fell into disrepute and lesser use at a time when it became apparent that individuals who were apparently steeped in these approaches were more likely to be consumed by narcissistic attention to their own agency and needs.

In other words, the criticism leveled against humanistic education has been that it promotes self-absorption. If this is the outcome, then it should no longer be described as humanistic. Humanism is attentive to human sensitivity and sensibility, both individually and collectively, and is demonstrated by care and attention to self and others. I like the description of humanism by Schneider and Leitner (2002) "as a dialectic between profound self inquiry, and inquiry into the world" (p. 3).

Patterson (Summer, 1987) outlines four reasons for the failure of humanistic education to be embraced in schools and teacher education:

1. Humanistic education became essentially a matter of introducing structured, teacher directed and controlled—games, exercises and other contrived experiences... no doubt many teachers felt unable to, or insecure in facing students without a lesson plan, in an unstructured situation...Teachers are not prepared for this kind of teaching.
2. The movement to get back to the basics, to the 3 R's, has discouraged the humanizing of the classroom. It is widely assumed that concern with affective development and human relationships in the classroom is in conflict with cognitive development... The evidence is, however, that a classroom atmosphere conducive to the affective development of students leads to greater, rather than less, academic progress. (Aspy, 1972)
3. In some places, poor judgment has been used by school personnel in selecting materials for values clarification classes.
4. Those who object to any consideration of values or the personal or affective, emotional development of children in the schools are often affiliated with conservative religious groups, or the religious right... [T]hey inaccurately classify all humanists as atheists. (9–10)

Patterson's ideas, although written in 1987, seem consistent with current views about education.

Humanistic and transpersonal paradigms are process-oriented. A process-oriented approach acknowledges and accepts life on its terms, as it is.

To accept does not imply either "liking" or "disliking" nor does it imply no effort to change. It means literal acceptance of what is, no more and no less. Process orientation is a perspective that is inclusive, sees the blending and interconnection of all things, and accepts of change as central to life. Process orientation follows experience as it unfolds. It stands as an alternative to rule-bound approaches that attempt to control human expression and creativity, what is natural, and that which marginalizes significant aspects of human experience. Process orientation is inclusive of goal achievement and production and is interested in how this fits with the natural rhythms of persons and of all of life. Sensitivity, caring, and relationality are valued. In a process-oriented approach, all positions are acknowledged as worthy of consideration, and dialogue at multiple levels and between seemingly incommensurate positions is facilitated.

HUMANISTIC PEDAGOGY

The very essence of a humanistic pedagogy, which is a phenomenologically based approach, is that it is responsive to human experience in concrete and in-the-moment ways. This responsiveness requires an educator who is developing an ever-refining sensitivity and fluidity of awareness and perception and who is response capable in the moment. Humanistic educators address students directly as human beings, create conditions where personal transformation is possible, work with the classroom as a community in development, and address curriculum content as part of a transformative learning process.[17] This direct and foremost attention to the human being in front of us is a first principle of humanistic pedagogy. Krishnamurti (1953/1981), the great South Asian spiritual teacher, says "We know how to meditate, how to play the piano, how to write, but we have no knowledge of the meditator, the player, the writer" (p. 63). Humanistic pedagogy pays attention to what goes on in the learner, his or her intra-, inter-, and transpersonal dimensions of being and sees behavior, achievement, and productivity as outcomes of this attention.

A pedagogy that privileges what the student achieves more than who the student is invariably values the development of the intellect over and above the feeling. Many confuse intellect with intelligence. As Krishnamurti also states:

> There is a distinction between intellect and intelligence. Intellect is thought functioning independently of emotion, whereas, intelligence is the capacity to feel as well as to reason; and until we approach life with intelligence, instead of intellect alone, or with emotion alone, no political or educational system in the world can save us from the toils of chaos and destruction. (pp. 63–64)

Thinking and feeling are both important. When these two human capacities are integrated, this represents true intelligence in action. If pedagogy encompasses true intelligence, then knowing the person in all dimensions of their being is crucial. The bodily, the emotional, the sensual, the spiritual, and all other domains of human being are given attention that fits the person(s), the moment, and the overall context. Nothing of being human being is left out or neglected. This is the second principle of humanistic pedagogy.

The third principle is paying special attention to inner experience with the associated inner work (Cohen, 2005). As indicated previously, there is no learning without changes, and educationally justifiable change comes from each individual's self-transformation. All other changes are externally imposed and, hence, go against the very essence of humanistic pedagogy, which values and validates the person no matter what his or her qualifications are in terms of achievement. Transformation requires awareness of what actually goes on in consciousness. The humanistic pedagogue encourages, supports, and shows ways to work with awareness of inner experience for both educators and learners as part of everyday curriculum.

CURRICULUM LEARNING

To complement the humanistic approach, the pedagogical approach incorporates the idea that each learner has a unique and dominant way of learning. To attend to these differences, each class addresses the curriculum material by including some succinct lecture content, opportunities to discuss and ask questions about the lecture content, descriptions of how the conceptual material is transformed into practice, demonstration of a practice, and an opportunity to practice. So, students can learn through discussion, through watching, and through experience. As well, the attention to the group's process, individual's process, and interaction enhances interactions between learners. The likelihood of having the full attention of students is facilitated by the overall ethos of care that is manifest through attention to the human dimension and by the modeling that is provided about being human and demonstrated passion for subject matter.

An overriding principle in all aspects of classroom experience is the emphasis and attention to process, both as an observer and a participant. Human and curriculum learning experience are viewed as in motion. Instances of being stuck, "wrong," are all viewed as points to delve into and learn from. This is in opposition to the more mainstream view that the person has a disorder, is dumb, or needs to work harder. With a prospective perspective, there is always somewhere to go; sometimes it is onward, sometimes inward, sometimes backward, and sometimes just being at a place of no movement.

A CASE STUDY OF HUMANISTIC, TRANSPERSONAL, AND PROCESS-ORIENTED PEDAGOGY

In this and the next section, I describe a case study of humanistic, transpersonal, and process-oriented pedagogy. I use my teaching experience in a counseling theories class at a community college[18] as data, along with the recorded experience of students from their reflective journals and used with their permission. This very diverse class consisted of 18 adult learners, with an age range from late 20s to early 50s, and a cultural mix that included East Asian, South Asian, and South African heritages. As part of the requirements for the course, students were offered three different assignment options. Six students chose the option that involved writing personal reflections about their classroom experience, which form the basis for this essay. Excerpts from their work, with their permission, are used to illustrate the theory and practice employed during the course and to demonstrate the inner world of the learners. The hope of most educators is that a spark will ignite an ongoing process within students. I saw a lot of sparks emerging from these students.

Classes are set up to be—and invariably are—community development experiences. Reading the reflections of each of these students gives insight into the inner experience of a learner within this context. The assignment, along with the classroom atmosphere, gives support and encouragement to the learners to attend to these experiences. I believe that these writings will explicate the experience for others who are contemplating being in or who already are in school. I believe that they are also informative for educators, highlighting the inner experience of students and the educator and the importance of attending to these human experiences within the context of a generative environment.

Let me describe the atmosphere and environment of my classroom so that you will have a sense of the "container" within which possibilities of humanistic, transpersonal, and process-oriented teaching and learning can take place. The class is conducted in a seminar format (Cohen, 2004). Students sit in a circle. There is no intervening furniture. The first 30 minutes of every class is devoted to the group's process and for personal sharing at whatever level each individual wishes. There is no requirement to share anything. The purpose of this time is for students to get to know each other and for the group to have an optimal opportunity to develop as a community. I assume the role of facilitator and, from time to time, move out of this role overtly and become a participant. Students may talk about their experience in the moment, life events, personal responses to course material and experience, relationship issues within the group, and feedback for each other and me. The effect of this is to create a sense of group identity and belonging. As well, students develop increased capacity for self-awareness, a valuable ability in life and for counselors.

Each meeting of the class is structured in a consistent manner, as follows:

6:30–7:00   Group time (check in, group process, issues; personal and interpersonal, feedback, sharing, contact opportunities)

7:00–7:15	Questions regarding course content, structure, assignments, and so on
7:15–8:00	Lecture and discussion
8:00–8:20	Break
8:20–9:25	Experiential exercise related to theory
8:20–8:40	Description, demonstration, and debriefing
8:40–9:15	Experiential opportunity for class, debrief in dyads or triads
9:15–9:25	Group debrief
9:25–9:30	Closure (sharing of personal experience for the particular class, statements of what is unfinished, sharing of learning experiences; whatever you need to do or say to feel closure for the evening)

As stated earlier, the purpose of the structure is to create safety to support the development of community within the context of the classroom; to provide an opportunity to have an experience of deep democracy (Arnold Mindell, 1995, 2002); and to support deep learning of curriculum. Deep democracy employs methods that experientially include what is frequently marginalized in groups and communities. Each voice is invited in and valued for its contribution. As well, conflict is invited into the open in order to facilitate the integration that it offers and to crack the shell of that which is less authentic and open the doors to an increasingly authentic experience. There is a requirement for a diverse range of facilitation skills from the leader (Cohen, 2004).

The feedback from students about the initial process-oriented period of each class indicates that this experience is an important part of their learning about themselves and about the realities they will encounter as counselors. Themes of feeling validated, being encouraged to express their creativity, and personal growth are consistently highlighted.

THEORY INTO PRACTICE: PERSONAL NARRATIVES AND REFLECTIONS

I was particularly challenged by the unusual amount of silence that occurred in the opening 30 minutes with this particular group—30 minutes that is devoted to instigating the creation of community within the classroom by providing opportunity for students to share their personal experiences at whatever level they wish. It is my experience that there is the occasional silence in this portion of the classes that I lead, but this group was unusually quiet. I work with silence in a variety of ways. I make the point that words are one of many possible ways of communicating and that we do not need to speak to get value from this process time. I keep the topic of silence in the foreground and encourage the group to speak and reflect about this recurrent phenomenon. At times, I found myself wondering what I was missing. At the eighth class, it occurred to me that the "ghost" of meditation was possibly present and not acknowledged, that is, the group essentially wanted to go inward and be introverted and silent. The idea of ghosts or ghost roles (Arnold Mindell, 1995) is that they represent roles or atmospheres that affect a group and that are not owned for any number of reasons. In this case, the reason being that neither I nor anyone in the class had to that point identified the desire of the group to be validated and encouraged in their desire to go inward and meditate rather than be overtly expressive. This experience highlights the powerful propensity that exists in education to privilege verbal expression and to marginalize silence and other forms of experience and communication, including movement, nonverbal contact, or performative activities such as art and music. This was an important learning occasion for me and, as you will see, a point of reflection for the student writers.

Perhaps most importantly, the writing contained here demonstrates the passion of students for learning about themselves, each other, and the subject matter. It seems evident to me that given the opportunity, students will engage in depth and breadth with that which is deeply meaningful for them. It is, perhaps, telling that each of these students went over the suggested limit for the assignment, and I believe you will discern from reading excerpts that this assignment absorbed them in a way that I believe is rare in educational experiences.

From here on, I will identify themes that emerged, share some student reflections along with my own, give some examples of pedagogical practice, and I will also provide some analytic and conceptual commentary.

BEGINNING[19]

CAROL: Expecting to spend three hours taking copious notes, the first class of my Counselling Theories course was a pleasant surprise. Desks were pushed to the perimeter of the classroom and our chairs arranged in a circle; I felt comfortable with this configuration as I've participated in various groups that used the same arrangement. Unlike linear, there is no beginning or end to the circle—I knew this formation removed any physical barriers between participants allowing interaction but more importantly, established our instructor as a facilitator/participant as opposed to an authoritarian (power-over) standing above students consciously or unconsciously sharing his knowledge and wisdom.

AVRAHAM: In my life as a student, I have been in classrooms that attempted to develop an egalitarian view and failed; others that were fairly successful; many that worked from the dominant paradigm, for example, the teacher is the authority and the only "real" holder of knowledge, with even some of those being at least a good enough experience; and I have been in classes where the instructor was clearly taking the authority position and that did not work very well at all for me.

When I think of deeply democratic environments (Arnold Mindell, 2002) that truly attend to "awareness of the diversity of people, roles, and feelings, and a guesthouse attitude toward whatever comes to the door of one's attention" (p. vii), I feel a sense of excitement and anticipation. This is what I attempt to propagate, and Carol's reflection hints at the possibilities of this in my classroom at the beginning of the course. My experience in classrooms where I have introduced the practices of deep democracy and a guesthouse attitude is that I feel alive and involved, which is very different to how I have felt in teacher-centered classrooms, where I feel much more dissociated, as if I am an observer or part of the audience. In those classrooms power, control, and knowledge "resides" in the teacher. It is not a multidimensional learning experience for me. I am, at best, a passive participant and, at worst, not involved at all. This is, however, reminiscent of my experiences as a high school student where I would frequently wile away the hours in my inner world, "skiing" the slopes of Whistler Mountain while my teacher attended to other things. This was actually a great learning opportunity for me about the power of visualization and imagination— too bad that was not the identified curriculum.

ANNIKA: Walking into session two was interesting, one of the students was busy re-organizing the room in a circle contradictory to what the instructor wanted in session one. She really wanted the desks in front of the chairs. She said she liked something to rest on and organize her papers and books. Every student there was keen on having desks in front of them, the instructor wanted no desk in front of people no barriers. The desks were removed and once again we sat exposed, facing each other. The discomfort of most people in the room was palpable, more so than in session one. What amazed me was that most people sat in exactly the same spot as in session one, me included. I wondered why that was. After reflection, I realized that as I was not at all sure what my place was in the group yet or how I fitted in. I knew that my physical body was in this area of the room in the first session and I had enjoyed session one.

AVRAHAM: I certainly relate to being an observer of process and dynamics as Annika is. I also relate to being for and against various classroom approaches. I liked the opportunity to encounter the "protest" movement, to demonstrate that I would hold the line on structure, and to use the experience as grist for our learning mill.

THE GUEST HOUSE

A poem from the Sufi tradition (Rumi, 1995) describes the guest house attitude that I hope to encourage in my classrooms:

The Guesthouse

This being human is a guest house.
Every morning a new arrival.

A joy, a depression, a meanness,
some momentary awareness comes
as an unexpected visitor.

Welcome and entertain them all;
even if they're a crowd of sorrows,
who violently sweep your house
empty of its furniture,
still, treat each guest honorably.
He may be clearing you out
for some new delight.

The dark thought, the shame, the malice,
meet them at the door laughing,
and invite them in.

Be grateful for whoever comes,
because each has been sent
as a guide from beyond. (p. 109)

SYLVIA: A woman in our class shares a beautiful story. I listen carefully to what she is saying but also realize that sharing is something that does not come easily. English is her second language and I believe she is very nervous of public speaking as her voice shakes when she speaks. Yet, here she is facing her fears and makes our experience in this class richer, well mine anyway. After she finishes I am compelled to thank her and let her know that I look forward to her stories every class. I didn't tell her this because I knew she was nervous but rather because I was truly moved by her story and appreciated her sharing with us. At the end of class the woman thanks me for my comment and said that it helped her. I am pleased that by my simple words of thanks had meant so much to her.

AVRAHAM: I am pleased to see that the guest-house attitude and responsibility is shared and that a student feels empowered that she has something of value to offer. I am also aware of how my "load" is lightened by this type of event. I am also touched as the woman who shared the story has struggled so hard to bring herself into the class as fully as possible. I also identify with her because I have known extreme shyness and fear of being seen in classrooms.

MID-LIFE RETURN TO SCHOOL

CAROL: In my experience as a mature student, apprehensiveness, curiosity, risk and vulnerability are experienced during the first class of most courses, yet it appears that the new physical demographics of our class increase the level of such feelings. As few students volunteer to speak I sense a general reservation within our group and recall my apprehension when I first participated in a group experience; I remember feeling anxious, vulnerable and exposed. The experience reminded me of how fearful I felt when I first stepped out of my comfort zone ending a destructive long-term relationship.

AVRAHAM: I certainly recall my experiences when I first returned to school after an absence of about 25 years. I did well, but I wondered why it took me so long to remember material. Was I losing my memory? I was somehow convinced that everyone else was much quicker and that I had lost a large number of my IQ points. When I returned the second time, I was surprised and felt that there must be some mistake when my graduate advisor in my MA counseling program referred to me as a top student. It really didn't occur to me that he might be saying what he believed. I recall, similar to the previous student, the gradual development of confidence that occurred within me as I realized that, indeed, not only could I do this but also that I was actually good at it. To this day even after being awarded a number of scholarships and much success with publication and conference presentations, I can still find within myself thoughts about how I am really not that good. At times these thoughts take over, and at other times I just watch them go by. A quirky little self within me pipes up, "Who do you think you are? It's only a matter of time until you are discovered."

SYLVIA: Our instructor wants us in a large circle to start the class and I find myself instantly uncomfortable. "How am I going to take notes properly? Where am I going to put my water and my coffee? If I can not look at the instructor then who am I going to look at? I hope we only do this for today."

We briefly go around the room and introduce ourselves and get to know each other a little bit. Well, you know, my name is, I do this for a living and perhaps mention why we are taking the course. I laugh inside because this seems to be the norm. We describe ourselves by our names and what we do.

We then turn to the course outline and as we are going over the three assignment choices I start to get butterflies in my stomach. I frantically read over them and start to panic! "I can't do that one! Oh my gosh that is due in two weeks! That one I have to be creative...five pages of creative, I suck at being creative." All of my fears of school and homework come rushing back. "What am I doing here? Do I really want to spend the next 8 plus years going back to school? Wouldn't it just be easier to stay where I am?" (I now know that reading about cognitive therapy before the course outline would have perhaps been helpful). "STOP and take a deep breath." I calm my racing brain and decide to go with the assignment I am the most afraid of. Why?

I get in my car to drive home and as always I am excited and full of energy. My mind goes over what we have just been taught, the people I have just met, and eagerly await the next week.

AVRAHAM: I am again reminded of my return to school, twice actually—once after 16 years and again after a further 10 years. The second time was to complete an MA in counseling. I was part of a cohort that was together for 2 1/2 years. The experience on both occasions was vivid. The first was of lesser importance as I had decided to dabble in kinesiology but still sufficient to raise my anxiety. The second was of major importance to me, as I saw that my future in my field would be affected by how I fared. I still recall my fearfulness on the first night of classes. Again, I was convinced that everyone was much better prepared than I was. I doubted my ability to learn and to perform. My memories from my undergraduate years were not particularly positive. I doubted my abilities as a student even though I had done well in my last year and in my brief sojourn as a kinesiology student. I sat in the classroom wondering who all these people were, what I was doing there, and what the professor was going on about. Why did she keep saying that this would be a powerful experience for us and that it would bring up all kinds of issues? How could she know this, I wondered?

SILENCE

OLIVER: During our class check-in times the class during our half hour remains quiet and still, as a group we have discussed this and tried to "figure out" why we are so quiet. I reflect now what is to "figure out" as though I and we are judging the quiet and stillness, versus conversations as right and wrong. Do I judge most of life against right and wrong? I think not, however it is possible that my bias is towards this.

CAROL: Silence, speech can be muted—thoughts are never silent. SILENCE—it's not enough to choose my words carefully, equally as important, definitely more concealed and probably more frequent, are my thoughts.

I wonder how silent Freud was. What's the reasoning behind our collective silence each week? Do we object to intrusion into our personal lives? Over a century later, we are not that unlike Freud expecting our clients to bare their souls while we remain silent.

OLIVER: I arrive and the class has begun, this arriving late I ask myself what is it about arriving late that makes me so uncomfortable, it seems to take me some time to get into what the class is talking about, as I listen I hear voices in my head telling me that the other students are much smarter than I am, they are getting this more than I am. These are the negative voices the committee of assholes in my brain trying to keep me stuck, keep me from moving ahead in my life...

I have a head ache as I enter class, I had a massage today and a head ache is some of the result. I am distracted in class by my pounding head, I would like to be more present for this class... acceptance, can I accept people where they are at? At this moment can I accept where I am at? Distracted and annoyed, unsettled with my head ache. How am I at accepting my lot in life? Jesus said "love your neighbor as yourself." How can I accept others where they are at and for who they are, if I am not accepting of my space, and time, and place in this life?

AVRAHAM: I was severely tested with this experience of silence in the class. I ran out of things to say about it. I had trouble living up to my belief that silence is okay. Eventually, I noticed my tendency to withdraw into my inner world, and it occurred to me that, perhaps, this is what the group wants to do—withdraw into their inner world. I decided to offer a period of meditation to open up the next class. The effect was magical. The group immediately accepted the offer, and when the meditation period was over, the group demonstrated an increased energy that manifested as sharing about their experiences meditating and other relevant life experiences.

AUTHENTICITY

JANICE: If I had to describe to someone the process that has occurred within me over the course of my time as a student of Counselling, I would be challenged to find words sufficient to truly define the experience. The experience has not been merely a bunch of moments strung together, which is so often how we think of our lives, "remember the time when such and such occurred," but rather it is as if a spark has ignited an ongoing process in me. A process that has been profound in many ways; it has progressed and retreated, it has challenged me and left me limp, it has engaged and disengaged me all at the same time and yet differently. What is even more interesting is that the process contains a sense of perpetual continuity if I choose to "be" with it. It's kind of like, once you come this far, you can't really go back. The process continues to challenge my awareness in each moment, to live authentically, to strive for "realness" within the moments I have with others but more starkly, to learn from every experience I have. I have come to recognize through my study that all channels (to borrow a word from the Process Counselling theories) of my experience make up the whole of my experience and that I must pay attention to all facets be they joyous or challenging——each experience provides an opportunity for insight.

AVRAHAM: What is my experience in this moment? I sit here. I type these words. I am getting quite tired. It is after 11:00 p.m., and I have had a full day, and tomorrow will be another full day. I hear words, "keep going" and other words, "go to bed." Who speaks? I am listening to folk music as I write. I have loved this form of music from my earliest encounter with it in my late teens. I recall my mother telling me to "turn off that noise" as I listened to the Free Wheeling Bob Dylan. "Don't think twice, it's all right. And it ain't no use to sit and wonder why babe. It don't make no difference anyhow." Formative sounds and words. Something in this music, the words, and the gravelly sound of his voice hit a profound place in me. I knew, at least for a moment, that I was not alone. I identified with the youth culture that longed for authenticity and connection. I found it, but then the dream died, or at least it seemed to, but I eventually realized that the dream may have died, but the dreamer that I am had not. That dreamer still exists.

ANNIKA: First day of Class, we are given a paper titled "Contemplations On and Rumors About the Inner Life of the Educator" written by the

Class instructor... I realized it was a personal account and felt engaged. I lifted my head as I realized that the person revealing their thought and feeling in this paper was sitting right there and I realized, with a fair bit of anxiety, that I would to some extent have to disclose myself to these strangers, who had just introduced themselves to all of us gathered in a circle. The anxiety was mixed with the excitement of the start of something new, another Journey.

AVRAHAM: As I read these reflections, I am picturing both of these students. I can see in my inner vision an image that is constituted by my felt sense of them as participants in the class. I recall my initial feeling in the class, wondering how this group would be; how they would respond to my approach; and how the class as a whole would be in its work together. I felt a mix of excitement and nervousness.

I wondered, and worried a little, if they would be actively involved or alternatively, reticent, critical, and separate. I realize as I write that these three words are reflections of my classroom experience and run all the way back to my experiences in high school and as an undergraduate. I became increasingly fearful as I grew older in educational environments. I recall dropping out of language classes repeatedly in my early years at university. I was terrified about speaking out in class. I remember my initial experience of a faltering performance in a grade 12 English class. I had no awareness of anything unusual. I was called upon to read. I stood up. As I began, I was aware that my voice was very shaky. I felt simultaneously an overpowering heat and an immense fragility. I had no idea what was happening. I felt as if I was watching something happen to someone else. Somehow I got through this experience. I was never again as I had been previous to this experience. As a younger child I had always relished the opportunity to read publicly. I was a good reader and enjoyed the appreciative comments that came my way. I recall in grades five and six being chosen to participate in children's programs on the CBC, experiences that I greatly enjoyed. It is clear to me now that I bring both dimensions from my past to my present teaching experience.

ALIENATION AND FEAR

OLIVER: The room starts to fill now with class mates. I feel distant and alone, this is a comfort zone I know all too well. As the class reconvenes from the break I notice I have pushed my chair and myself out of the circle. I am disconnected with the group and in some ways with myself. I ask myself, "How much of this baggage belongs to another time, or another person or another place?"

SYLVIA: Our instructor joins our session just as I start to be the counselor, oh goodie. I do not really want him to observe but say to myself, "take advantage of his knowledge and what you can learn from him observing." I continue with our session and a very interesting experience happens where the use of Gestalt therapy works well. While I am doing this I have that terrible little voice talking away in the background, but yet ever so present killing my confidence. Reminding me that here are two people that I sometimes find intimidating, watching me. En guard, my other little voice comes out armed saying "Get over it...don't care so much...who cares what they think." In the end, the best voice wins. I didn't look as stupid as I thought I would. It was an excellent learning experience.

OLIVER: I arrive and the class has begun, this arriving late I ask myself what is it about arriving late that makes me so uncomfortable, it seems to take me some time to get into what the class is talking about, as I listen I hear voices in my head telling me that the other students are much smarter than I am, they are getting this more than I am. These are the negative voices the committee of assholes in my brain trying to keep me stuck, keep me from moving ahead in my life...

I have a head ache as I enter class, I had a massage today and a head ache is some of the result. I am distracted in class by my pounding head, I would like to be more present for this class...acceptance, can I accept people where they are at? At this moment can I accept where I am at? Distracted and annoyed, unsettled with my head ache. How am I at accepting my lot in life? Jesus said "love your neighbor as yourself." How can I accept others where they are at and for who they are, if I am not accepting of my space, and time, and place in this life?

AVRAHAM: I have been a reflective person for as long as I can recall. I remember lying in my bed as a child of about 10. My parents were away. The housekeeper had invited someone over. They were loud. I was frightened. My brother slept in the next bed, obliviously. I was paralyzed with my fear. My small body was no doubt tense and quivering, but in those days I had already learned to not identify my body's sensations. I was thinking about how I could escape to my beloved child sitter, who lived only one house away, and who represented safety and security. Our bedroom was on the second floor of our two-story house. I recall thinking that I could, perhaps, shinny down the drain pipe. Fortunately, I did not attempt this. Something in me learned that I was alone with my experience and that there was nobody to tell. This was an early inner reflection and also formative. I did tell my parents when they returned and the housekeeper was soon gone, but the tracks of character formation that would nurture my fearful thoughts and feelings were laid down even as my propensity for inner dialogue was supported.

CONSCIOUSNESS TRANSFORMATION

The inner life experiences described here are representative of what actually goes on inside educators and students and are demonstrative of the psychological atmosphere in classrooms. The depth and breadth of what is occurring below the surface in classrooms and the effect that this has on individuals, the collective, and on learning is explicated. Also demonstrated is how the encouragement of inner and personal reflection practice, along with various forms of expression, facilitates personal growth, classroom community development, and the learning of curriculum material.

Educators' conceptions of teaching fall along a continuum. At one end of the continuum, they function much like some kind of radio transmitter, broadcasting information, and like a radio, having no capacity to recognize the presence or absence of student responses or lack of responses. On the other end of the continuum are educators who are deeply committed to themselves and their students as human beings individually and in interaction with one another. Educators need to be able to work at various points along the continuum in ways that are responsive to the moment, sensitive to the students in the room, and the larger context.

I believe educators are caught in a bind. If they aren't able to deal with this multidimensionality of human consciousness and human personality, they must still construct a response, no matter how inadequate. If they do acknowledge that developing the necessary skills and metaskills (Cohen, 2002; Amy Mindell, 1994/2001), the in-the-moment feeling attitudes that are reflective of an educator's most deeply held values, attitudes, and sense of identity, then they have taken a major step toward acknowledging and engaging the human dimension in their classrooms. I believe this is essential to masterful pedagogic practice. These abilities are developed through inner work and lead to educators becoming sensitive, alert, relational, and authentic human beings.

Having read these reflections, both the students' and my own, I imagine that you have some sense of what the classroom experience was from both an inner world perspective and in relationship to classroom interaction. What conclusions can be drawn from these ruminations and reflections? I am suggesting that similar though different experiences are coursing through the consciousness of all students in all classrooms and that a failure to acknowledge these experiences is costly to individual students, the classroom community as a whole, and educators. The richness of these inner life experiences is what infuses classrooms with the life force that is meaningful and that simultaneously creates meaning. The collective experience, the sharing of that experience, and the awareness that such experience is valid and validated is akin to an infusion of the unbearable lightness of being, the sheer joy of existence, remembrance of the human potential to feel a deep sense of awe, and direct experience of the human spirit and the spirit that is beyond the human. The pathway to this experience is personal inner work that leads to an enhanced capacity for consciousness in the moment.

Krishnamurti's (1953/1981) idea of true intelligence is demonstrated along with the importance of being present in the moment. It is apparent that these students are thinking and feeling in an integrated way. As well, their sense of identity is emerging for them and others. A sense of the human within the academic community that is unusual in a classroom is part of their descriptions. Learning is embodied. Engagement with curriculum is lively.

The challenge for educators is to know themselves, to know their students, to have students know more about themselves and each other, to optimize the level of humaneness, to foster meaningful dialogue, and to integrate the personal and experiential with the curricular.

REFERENCES

Aspy, D. N. (1972). *Toward a technology for humanizing education.* Champaign, IL: Research.

Clarke, A. (1994). Student-teacher reflection: Developing and defining a practice that is uniquely one's own. *International Journal of Science Education, 16*(5), 497–509.

Cohen, A. (2002, May). The secret of effective psychotherapy: Metaskills. *The Private Practitioner Bulletin of the Canadian Counselling Association, 1*(3), 3–4.

Cohen, A. (2004). A process-oriented approach to learning process-oriented counselling skills in groups. *Canadian Journal of Counselling, 38*(3), 152–164.

Cohen, A. (2005). *Contemplations and rumours about the inner life of the educator: The gap between who we are and who we appear to be in classrooms.* Unpublished manuscript, University of British Columbia, Vancouver, Canada. (An earlier draft of this paper was presented at AERA 2005: Demography and Democracy in the Era of Accountability. Presentation to Spirituality and Education, SIG, under the title of *We teach who we are and that is the problem,* Montreal, QC, Canada.)

Hansen, D. (2005, September 6). 25% of youngest students not ready for classroom. *The Vancouver Sun,* p. 1.

Krishnamurti, J. (1981). *Education and the significance of life.* New York: Harper & Row. (Original work published 1953)

Meier, D. (2005, July/August). *Early childhood education at a crossroads: Voices from the field: Transforming the world of childhood in school.* Retrieved on July 20, 2005, from http://www.hel-earlyed.org/

Miller, J. P. (1996). *The holistic curriculum.* Toronto, ON: OISE.

Mindell, Amy. (1994/2001). *Metaskills: The spiritual art of therapy.* Portland, OR: Lao Tse Press.

Mindell, Arnold. (1995). *Sitting in the fire: Large group transformation using conflict and diversity.* Portland, OR: Lao Tse Press.

Mindell, Arnold. (2002). *The deep democracy of open forums: Practical steps to conflict prevention and resolution for the family, workplace, and world.* Charlottesville, VA: Hampton Roads.

Patterson, C. H. (1987, Summer). What has happened to humanistic education? *Michigan, Journal of Counseling and Development, XVIII*(1), 8–10.

Rumi. (1995). *The essential Rumi* (Coleman Barks, Trans.). New York: HarperCollins.

Schneider, K. J., & Leitner, L. M. (2002). Humanistic psychotherapy. In *The encyclopedia of psychotherapy* (Vol. 1, pp. 949–957). New York: Elsevier Science. Retrieved on June 29, 2006, from http://www.psybc.com/pdfs/library/Humanistic_Psychotherapy1.pdf (p. 3)

AFTERWORD:
THE CONTINUING BEGINNING

Wind
A student says,
I feel a still warm wind, and
My longing reaches toward you.

An educator says,
I feel a still warm wind, and
My longing reaches toward you.
——a. cohen

Writing this manuscript has simultaneously been akin to both being and meeting the invisible still warm wind. The writing has provided me an unparalleled opportunity to clarify and grow my ideas about education, educators, human beings, and life. At times, I felt more like a vehicle for a transmission that was more about energy than content. I wrote about things that I have discovered, and I discovered things as I wrote.

I brought practice into my writing, and the discoveries that occurred there translated into my practice. I have lived the experiences that are contained here. Their roots grew from seeds that were planted long ago. I feel the connection between all things out of which this work has grown. There are more things contained here than I could ever say or even know, and yet I know that they are here.

Suffering in classrooms mirrors the suffering in the world and in individual humans. My writing is about what I have discovered in my personal and professional life that has enhanced my ability to address life, including suffering, as it is. On the material and conditional levels, life is full of events that bring joy, suffering, and everything in between. The Buddhist view states that this is the nature of human existence. I believe that there is a possibility at the essence level, the pure ground of being and nonbeing, emptiness (mushin[20]), the nagual[21], within the field of the Dao, or whatever name you choose to apply, where life is experienced differently. I don't know if it is possible to live in this state of consciousness all the time. I know it's possible to live there at moments. I have learned that it is possible to become increasingly proficient at accessing those moments and bringing them into everyday life. My writing is really about bringing the pure ground of being to life in classrooms.

I have attempted to describe the theory, practice, and praxis of a pedagogy that encourages educators to be authentic and encouraging in life and to see education as a vibrant undertaking. I have drawn upon the discipline of counseling from humanistic, existential, transpersonal, group, and process-oriented perspectives. The essence of these approaches acknowledges the humans, the intersubjective, nonhuman, spiritual, and an ongoing attitude and practice of inquiry toward life. I have also drawn upon holistic and humanistic educational perspectives. I have drawn upon Eastern philosophy substantially and western philosophy a little. I have invited these different perspectives into the conversation about education as I believe that they add important new ideas.

What follows are dimensions of human experience that are either developing or not in a person in relationship to an emergent metacommunicator and that are descriptive of crucial areas for development in an educator, and that have appeared thematically through this manuscript:

1. *Exuberance:* the capacity to feel and express fully the sheer joy and awe of being alive.
2. *Poignancy:* the capacity to deeply and fully feel the pathos of life.
3. *Curiosity:* the drive to investigate the world.
4. *Wu-wei:* the capacity for creative emptiness; optimal energy use.
5. *Awareness:* the capacity to be self-aware; to observe experience.
6. *Expression:* the capacity to express thoughts and feelings to another.
7. *Receptivity:* the capacity to receive thoughts and feelings from another.

Educators without sufficient awareness and capability in these domains are less than fully engaged in life, and, so will, to use that somewhat worn-out phrase, teach who they are, the "who" that is less than optimal for them and for their students. That identity is one that sends a conflicting message—the age old one of dissonance. There might be talk about paradigm shifts, but all too quickly it becomes apparent that this is rhetoric and not practice. There is ample evidence from the fields of psychotherapy that demonstrates the effect of conflicting messages. Mice put in situations where no matter what they did they would be shocked and where the shocks were unpredictable eventually went into a state of withdrawal, developed skin lesions, and became immobilized. Students who are subjected to capricious and unpredictable messages from educators, no matter how kindly and well intended those educators are, will begin to manifest similar, though not always overtly visible, reactions. They will be reminded consciously or unconsciously of any similar experiences in their own personal history, they may be moved to a personal edge, and may manifest their usual and survival-oriented response that manifests unconsciously and as tuning out in the moment. Their learning and liveliness is adversely affected to an extreme. Witnessing the world, I can only say that it is working. Dissonance is a strongly realized, unacknowledged value in education and the world. Of course, the potential to use these experiences as an ally to become more of who they are also exists in these difficult situations.

Alice Miller (1981/1994) writes about the effects of dissonance on children: "We are all prisoners of our childhood, whether we know it, suspect it, deny it, or have never even heard about the possibility" (p. 25). Peter Schellenbaum (1988/1990) states, "The unloved think they've been abandoned by the entire world" (p. 163). Both of these authors described the tragic and deep loneliness of the unloved. The feeling of being cut off from the world and other human beings is a tragic and devastating experience of dissonance. Another way of characterizing this experience is incongruity, which is the dissonance between what is said and what is done. This is confusing and soul damaging to a child. The child will interpret dissonance as meaning that he or she is unloved and unlovable. This arises out of the relational gap that exists between the child and those adults who are most significant. Eventually, the personality and behavioral patterns that emerge in response to being unloved become the barriers between the person and their authentic self, between them and another person, and between them and all of life. These experiences are happening all the time in classrooms within both educator and learners.

The seven dimensions outlined previously are basic ways of being for an awakening educator and underpin the threads detailed next that exemplify the paradigm shift and focus of educators who are aiming for such a shift:

1. Self → Self-Other
   Focus moves from only individual to both individual and relational and includes the notion of tendencies to focus on self and other but within the context of Self-Other.
2. Utility of Relationship → I-Thou Encounter
   Focus moves from utility to the relationship encounter as an end in itself and does not exclude the possibility of utility as part of the encounter.
3. Heart vs. Mind Dichotomy → Heart/Mind/Body/Spirit/Community

Shift from binary view of Heart and Mind to an integrated experience of Heart, Mind, Body, Spirit, and Community.

4. Consumption → Sustainability
   Shift from consumption and production to a long-range view of what will sustain processes over time.

5. I am not That → I am That (there is nothing that I am not)
   A shift in the tendency to dis-identify completely from that which is considered negative and toward recognizing that all potentials exist within a human being. This does not mean that those potentials need to be acted upon.

6. Doing → Being
   A shift in consciousness and activity from emphasis on activity and production to a focus on being, being present in the moment with awareness across the continuum of innerprivate experience to that which is located in the outer world, and a recognition that these dimensions are on a continuum and not separated.

7. Information Consumption → In Touch with Others and Otherness
   Re-orientation to the human who is conveying information as central and connection to otherness and away from seeing humans as fleshy technology that excretes information.

8. Anomy and Alienation → Touching
   A shift from separation and dissociation to touching of the world, human and nonhuman, physically, emotionally, and/or spiritually.

9. Expedience → Community Enhancement
   A shift in perspective and values from "whatever works" to "how does this affect the community in its entirety."

10. Measurement and Counting → Ecological Dimension
    A shift in criteria from measuring and counting to a valuing of and concern for the ecological dimension, including the human impact of an activity on the overall ecology.

11. Clock Time → Timelessness (Presence)
    A move in consciousness from concern about the future and worry about the past to being fully present—an experience of timelessness.

12. Maximum Speed → Optimal Pace
    A shift from valuing fastest to valuing optimal pace—the pace that
    fits the person, others, and the total context.

13. Accelerative → Organic
    Recognition that a constant focus on accelerated rates of produc-
    tion are neither respectful to the humans involved and the overall
    environment nor profitable to a focus on noticing signals that sug-
    gest constant fine-tuning of pace to suit all aspects of the context.

Attending to these threads requires an alertness that implies being
consciously present, noticing what is actually there, noticing the meaning that emerges, and following the indicated course of action, or inac-
tion. This type of process is not a strategy. No two moments are the
same. No two learnings are the same. No person is the same as they
were an instant ago. Education for presence in the moment seems crucial. Development of my observing self, my metacommunicator, is also
crucial. Educators who are awake in the moment model presence and
every-moment aliveness and full potential for learning. This is the greatest teaching that an educator can offer students.

I have made metaphoric and descriptive allusions to classrooms that
are in the flow of life as opposed to those that seem committed to "force
feeding" behavior and bits of information to learners. As Elizabeth Morley (2006) said, "We don't need bits of knowledge. We have Google
for that." Being in the field of Dao in an educational environment for me
means knowing in a substantial way what the context, content, and atmosphere of the environment are in the moment, each moment. The process
is important for the richness of each step along the way and the learning
that occurs through experiencing that process.

The first chapter of the *Dao De Jing* (Lao Tsu, 1972/1989) suggests
that whatever you can say—meaning conceptualize—about it, that is,
the Dao is not what it is. In the way that a map is not territory and the
finger that points to the moon is not the moon, all of our conceptualiza-
tions, no matter how extensive and articulate, are still not experience.
The *Dao De Jing* consistently reminds us of this message, an important

one for educators. The *Dao De Jing* reaches across time and cultural divides, languages, and translation differences. Next is the first verse of the *Tao Te Ching* (Lao Tzu, 2001). On the right is my rendering of chapter 1 related to educational experience:

Verse 1	**Living Inquiry 1**
A way that can be walked	There is an energy that precedes and is
is not the Way	intrinsic to all action, intention,
A name that can be named	corporeality, and materiality.
is not The Name	
Tao is both Named and Nameless	This energy can be spoken of but this speak-
As Nameless, it is the origin of all things As	ing must not be confused with the energy,
Named, it is the mother of all things	which by definition must be experienced
A mind free of thought,	directly to be known.
merged within itself,	
beholds the essence of Tao	Thoughts that take possession of
A mind filled with thought,	consciousness will necessarily obscure the
identified with its own perceptions,	Dao—
beholds the mere forms of this world	The lifeforce that animates all things.
Tao and the world seem different	
but in truth they are one and the same	Dao and the world are continuous.
the only difference is what we call them	The world is the Dao in form,
How deep and mysterious this unity is	And the Dao is both the precursor and pres-
how profound, how great!	ent in form.
It is the truth beyond the truth,	
the hidden within the hidden	Description of Dao tends toward removal
It is the path to all wonder	from Dao.
the gate to the essence of everything!	Living the Dao in the moment is True.
(p. 14)	

Many people have the "ability" to tune out their experiences in the inner and outer worlds. This ability, which might be more accurately described as a disability, develops out of experience as described previously by Miller and Schellenbaum. Some do not develop this ability. These people are often seen as visionaries, lunatics, or troublemakers. Personally, I feel a resonance with these timespirits. I believe that those educators who do not tune out, who are conscious and aware, are the educators that inspire students personally and academically. In their classrooms, education is a finely integrated mix of the personal, the experiential, and curriculum.

I have become increasingly convinced that lack of consciousness, awareness in the moment, is consistent with psychic numbing (Vetlesen, 1994), which goes hand-in-hand with intellectual and emotional shutting down and explains lack of sensitivity to others and an inability to learn. Sensitivity and awareness in the moment are integrally connected. The educator's awareness and sensitivity need to be in a process of opening and becoming increasingly responsive to self and other(s), including the otherness of the nonhuman. I am convinced that true education is intrinsically connected to the development of consciousness and relationship. The possibilities in educational environments for connection and learning about connection are immense. To the extent that connection occurs and consciousness develops, a classroom is a place of integrated learning about curriculum and being human. The following is attributed to the Zen sage Bodhidharma:

> A special tradition outside the scriptures
> No dependence upon words and letters;
> Direct pointing at the heart of man,
> Seeing into one's own nature, one attains Buddhahood.
>
> (Batchelor, 2001, p. 35)

Bodhidharma's words point me to the heart, toward my nature, toward the heart of being, but even more so, life points me in this direction. Life in classrooms is a rare and too-often-missed opportunity to be guided or pointed in this direction. The effort to live in this way is fruitful and contributes to compassion for self and others.

This book outlines many possibilities for the practice of education both in theory and practice and for the uncovering of the gifts that lie within any educator or preservice educator. The ideas described here have radical implications for the education of teachers. This writing is the transition point to the next step in my work, the inquiry into a relatively unexplored area, exemplary educators, the nurturance of the gifts within all educators, and a broad and thorough inquiry into the most important of works, the development of educators who have the immense and crucial responsibility to grow the future.

Breeze
I blow through you
Leaving no trace
Yet you know I've been here.

—Lao-Tzu's child[22]
—a. cohen

ILLUSTRATION 3. *Friends.*

© 2008, photograph by Lumina Romanycia.
Reproduced with permission from Lumina Romanycia.

REFERENCES

Batchelor, M. (2001). *Zen*. London: Thorsons.

Castaneda, C. (1972). *Journey to Ixtlan: The lessons of Don Juan*. New York: Simon and Schuster.

Lao Tsu. (1989). *Te Tao Ching* (Gia-Fu Feng & Jane English, Trans.). Toronto, ON, Canada: Vintage Books. (Original work published 1972)

Lao Tzu. (2001). *Tao Te Ching: The definitive edition* (J. Star, Trans.). New York: Jeremy P. Tarcher/Putnam.

Miller, A. (1981/1994). *The drama of the gifted child: The search for the true self*. New York: HarperCollins.

Morley, E. (2006, February 16). *Keynote address*. Presented at the WestCast Conference 2006: Languages of Learning, Vancouver, BC, Canada.

Sekida, K. (2003). *A guide to Zen: Lessons from a modern master* (M. Allen, Ed.). New York: Weatherhill. (Original work published 1985)

Schellenbaum, P. (1990). *The wound of the unloved: Releasing the life energy* (T. Nevill, Trans.). Dorset, U.K.: Element Books. (Original work published 1988)

Vetlesen, A. J. (1994). *Perception, empathy, and judgment*. University Park: Pennsylvania State University.

ENDNOTES

1. These lines, including the source, emerged spontaneously during my regular practice of meditation on the morning of March 19, 2006. Meditation is, for me, a playful and creative practice.
2. Retrieved on March 10, 2008, from http://www.photoselections.com/hammatt.htm
3. By *authentic* I mean a congruence and an integration between what a person expresses and what is in his or her inner world. Further, I view this inner experience as reflective of something that is akin to what could be called his or her true nature. It is not just any inner experience. The Buddhists might say, "It is the face you had before you were born."
4. I have put substantial effort into finding the original source for this story, including http://flowidealism.blogspot.com/2004/06/mastering-art-of-living.html, from where I retrieved it on March 16, 2005, but it has eluded me.
5. Metaskills (Cohen, 2002; Amy Mindell, 1994/2001) are superordinate skills that reflect deeply held beliefs and values and are demonstrated by the in-the-moment feelings and attitudes that accompany the practice skills of the educator.
6. By *authentic*, I mean the following: that the expression of the person is very likely to be perceived as interconnected in terms of language, tone, pace, facial expression, and body movement/stillness. Further, it will be the case that this expression is consistent with deeply held beliefs, values, and sense of the person.
7. This witness consciousness is intrinsic to many wisdom traditions, including, Buddhism, Taoism, Sufism, and Christian contemplative traditions.
8. An extended demonstration of inner work is given in the essay, "Dreaming Life: Working With a Personal Dream—On My Own," on page 185.
9. I am indebted to Dr. Arnold Mindell (1995) for this term, which advances the idea of a role as something that exists at a particular time and place and that may or may not be embodied. By *embodied*, I mean someone actually taking ownership of the timespirit rather than it being talked about and being a ghost role—a role that is attributed to someone who is not present. The *boss* would be an example of this.
10. By *educator*, I mean the individual around whom learning is meant to take place and for learners around whom it does take place.

11. By *counselor*, I mean one who is performing the kinds of activities in the presence of another or others that evoke, provoke, and educe learning in the inter- and intrapersonal realms.

12. This emerged from the same source as endnote number 1, also in March 2006.

13. Reproduced with permission of Springer Publishing Company, LLC, New York, NY 20035. It previously appeared in 2004 in *Ethical Human Psychology and Psychiatry: An International Journal of Critical Inquiry*, 6(3), 217–230, under the title *Dissociative Identity Disorder: Perspectives and Alternatives*.

14. Retrieved in July 2002, from http://www.geocities.com/dreamiris2001/dictionary.htm#B

15. I am indebted to Dr. Karen Meyer for introducing me to this term, which I take to mean an inquiry that is alive, that is lived as a substantial life experience, and that continually opens to possibilities in the dimensions of time, place, language, and otherness.

16. This term that I have coined refers to the pharmaceutical industries, mental health services, and many in my profession of counseling.

17. John Miller (1996) described three pedagogical orientations: (1) transmission—a one-way relationship where the teacher imparts information to the students; (2) transaction—a cognitive interaction where there is a process of inquiry and problem solving involving interaction. It is essentially a conversation between the student and the curriculum; and (3) transformation—the suggestion here is that there are two types of change, one that focuses on the individual and another that focuses on the collective. Transformation means a change in the world view. Miller favors the transformation orientation and recognizes that all positions have their uses. I agree and suggest that additionally, educators need to address students directly as human beings, create conditions where personal transformation is possible, work with the classroom as a community in development, and address curriculum content as part of a transformative learning process.

18. I believe that the adult learners in my class "were" the children, now grown up, who suffered from "inhuman" and production-oriented education as children. I believe that the approach employed with them is different than it would be with children but that this difference is one of emphasis but not of substance. An advantage of working with adults for this project is that they are able to articulate their experience in a psychologically sophisticated and nuanced way.

19. All names have been changed. Names used are consistent with participant's gender and cultural background. With a few minor editing exceptions for clarity, I have left the writings of the students intact to preserve the integrity and feeling of their work. Permission to use these writings was given by the students and a Certificate of Approval for the research was granted by the Behavioral Research Ethics Board of the University of British Columbia.

20. "Literally this means 'no mind' (*mu,* no; *shin,* mind), which means 'no ego... the mind is in a state of equilibrium'" (Sekida, 1985/2003, p. 112).

21. In the works of Carlos Castaneda (1972), the nagual is the world of the spirit and is in contrast to the world of the tonal, which is the world of the everyday.

22. This utterance emerged from the same source as endnote number 1 in March, 2006.

INDEX